Trail Cooking

An Outdoor Life Book

Trail Cooking

▲▲▲▲▲▲▲▲▲▲▲▲▲▲▲▲▲▲▲▲▲▲▲▲▲

John Weiss

DRAWINGS BY TED BURWELL

Outdoor Life Books

Van Nostrand Reinhold Company

My thanks to the editors of *Petersen's Hunting and Camping Journal* for allowing me to reprint portions of Chapter 12, 13 and 14, which originally appeared in those magazines.

Published by

Outdoor Life Books
Times Mirror Magazines, Inc.
380 Madison Avenue
New York, NY 10017

Distributed to the trade by

Van Nostrand Reinhold Company
135 West 50th Street
New York, NY 10020

Library of Congress Catalog Card Number: 80-5888
ISBN: 0-442-29324-0

Manufactured in the United States of America

For Mike Wolter and Whitey
Ellard, two of the finest
trail cooks I've ever shared
a mess kit with.

Contents

▲▲▲▲▲▲▲▲▲▲▲▲▲▲▲▲▲▲▲▲▲▲▲▲▲▲▲▲▲▲

Preface

▲▲▲▲▲▲▲▲▲▲▲▲▲▲▲▲▲▲▲▲▲▲▲▲▲▲▲

There is an old saying that an army travels on its stomach, and I will verify it is true.

I can remember my infantry training days at Fort Dix, New Jersey, the weekly 10-mile hikes with rifles and full field packs, and the bivouacs we pitched in the woods. Mostly I remember the strenuous exercise in all extremes of weather — summer heat in excess of 100° and winter cold in the teens. More often than not we were a bedraggled-looking lot, either soaking wet, covered with mud, on the brink of heat prostration, or close to frostbite.

Despite such adverse conditions we nevertheless were able to complete our assignments in good health, if not always good spirits. And if any single explanation can be attributed to that success, I'll rate the mess tent at the very top of the list.

Of course, the grub wasn't fancy, but it was nutritious and geared to the high energy levels we required. And that combination was far more responsible for keeping us going than our army woolies or barking drill sergeants.

Since those army days, fifteen years have passed and I'm reminded of another maxim, about history repeating itself. I find myself again taking 10-mile hikes with a rifle and a full pack on my back, living in a small tent, and engaging in strenuous activities in all kinds of weather. I may be tracking a whitetail buck, or stalking a wild sheep with a telephoto lens, or searching for a remote alpine lake where wild trout have never seen an angler's lure. The nice thing about these trips is there's no chow line. Instead, I fend for myself by practicing the art of trail cooking.

Trail cooking is neither mysterious nor difficult to master.

Yet, as in the case of soldiering, wholesome food is important to the success and well being of sportsmen (and women) who hunt, fish, camp, or pursue other outdoor pastimes. How and what you eat greatly affects your health, stamina, and the enthusiasm with which you undertake various activities.

Trail cooking is somewhat tricky to define, as the wide choices among foods, methods of preparing them, and required equipment all depend largely on individual circumstances. Are you traveling alone or in the company of several others who can share the weight? Will you be penetrating a deep wilderness region on a ten-day jaunt and have to carry in the food for thirty meals, or merely taking a weekend trip requiring only four or five? To supplement meals, what foraging opportunities are likely to be available along the way? Is the journey to be entirely on foot or will you go at least part of the way by horseback or Jeep? The time of year and even the altitude play their roles too in determining which particular foods and cooking methods are most appropriate to the adventure in question.

With these points in mind, it's easy to see that trail cooking can mean many things to different people. But aside from these diverse considerations there also are many common threads that bind together basic trail-cooking concepts. Just one of them, the philosophy that underpins nearly all of the chapters to follow, is "light is right." Simplicity and efficiency are crucial elements as well. But perhaps one of the most important elements is that trail cooking is just plain fun.

In fact, in trying to recall hundreds of hunting or fishing trips, it often is difficult for me to remember the precise details of how I shot a certain deer or brought a nice fish to net. But gathering blackberries to make a pie in camp, baking sourdough biscuits in a reflector oven, or roasting venison underground in a dutch oven are experiences that seem to remain etched in memory. I am not exactly sure why this is so — maybe because so much of our existence centers around eating — but on the trail I find myself looking forward as eagerly to mealtime as any other activity. Learn the skills of trail cooking and you will, too.

JOHN WEISS
Chesterhill, Ohio

Trail
Cooking

1

▲▲ **1** ▲▲▲▲▲▲▲▲▲▲▲▲▲▲▲▲▲▲▲▲▲

Planning Meals and Menus

Our country was settled by trappers, Indian scouts, bounty hunters, surveyors, prospectors, railroad workers, dirt farmers, cowboys, lawmen, and even outlaws. Despite their widely different occupations, one thing they all had in common was the need to cook their meals in the outdoors.

Those repasts were plain. You carried your saddlebags into a mercantile and the storekeeper filled them with assorted cloth sacks. The customary purchase consisted of 10 pounds of flour, 10 pounds of dried beans, 5 pounds of coffee, 1 pound of salt, a tin of baking powder, and a slab of salt pork. You were now ready for another week on the trail, or until scurvy, rickets, or some other malady forced you to visit the sawbones at the nearest fort or settlement town.

Trail menus varied so little in those early times that you could distinguish between breakfast, lunch, and supper only by looking at your pocketwatch. The cooking itself was repetitious. First, render a bit of the salt pork in a cast iron skillet and then add a glop consisting of flour, water, salt, and baking powder. Stir vigorously, cover the pan with a lid, and in short order you had something vaguely resembling bread. Second, set the bread aside and add beans to the frypan along with some water, mix in the remains of the rendered pork crispings, and cook until arriving at the consistency of manzanita bark. Third, throw a handful of coffee beans into a battered lard pail, add water, bring to a boil, then save the beans for use again another time. Fourth, choke it all down while shuddering at the thought of the next meal, the same all over again, only hours away.

Now leap forward 100 years. The setting again is somewhere in the remote outback. You're huddled over a tiny aluminum stove that is generating an iridescent propane flame. You reach into your backpack and extract one plastic bag containing several others sealed in foil. The package is labeled "Breakfast, Day 1." Within minutes, and after little more effort than adding water to the contents of the various bags, you're enjoying scrambled eggs, hashbrown potatoes, pilot bread slathered with honey, orange juice, and delicious hot chocolate.

Sometime later, around noon, after giving both your legs and casting arm a good deal of exercise, you unwrap a 7-ounce package, "Lunch, Day 1," reconstitute it to its original size, and soon you're savoring a hearty vegetable beef soup, bolton biscuits, fudge brownies, and hot tea laced with cinnamon.

Still later, at dusk, the evening meal proves equally compelling. After less than 12 minutes' cooking time you're relishing turkey tettrazini, green beans, applesauce, crisp crackers, and, for dessert, a strawberry milkshake.

This is the culinary world of the modern trail tramper, given birth by means of space-age technology to provide today's outdoor buff with incredibly versatile cooking equipment and a host of lightweight foods that require little preparation time but almost deserve gourmet rating.

Modern trail cooks use space-age equipment and special, light-weight foods to produce meals that are both tasty and nutritious.

Great-grandfather may be entitled to reminisce fondly about "the good old days" when he could wander across endless miles of pristine wilderness and fish clear waters. But respectfully inform him that when it comes to tasty, nutritious food on the trail, the "good old days" are right now.

EMPHASIS ON NUTRITION

People come in all shapes and sizes, and day to day engage in a myriad of activities on the trail, so it is impossible to state the exact body fuel requirements for every individual or situation. Yet some generalities pertaining to food intake can be taken into account to help anyone to plan nutritious trail-cooking menus.

An average person, at home and following a regular workday routine, requires 2,000 to 2,500 calories per day, depending upon how active he is. On the trail, however, during even the mildest of weather conditions, a man or a woman will easily burn a minimum of 3,500 calories. During particularly strenuous outings they may burn 4,500 calories or more per day and yet arrive home at the end of the week to find themselves several pounds lighter.

No matter the activity, these necessary calories are derived from the foods we eat, so it is imperative to design meals not only around taste and convenience but of sufficient caloric value to meet our total daily requirements.

For brief periods on the trail (anything less than two weeks) a sportsman should be concerned about three basic food elements: carbohydrates, fats, and proteins. Vitamins and minerals are the other elements essential to good health, but there is really no need to worry about them during abbreviated outings since they are found in adequate quantities in balanced diets containing the other three. Yet if you regularly take vitamin supplements at home (especially in the case of iron for women), it's good to stick with your customary dosage on the trail; store what you'll need in a small, moistureproof pillbox.

Of the three basic elements, carbohydrate grams should comprise fifty percent of the total caloric requirements. Twenty-five percent should be in the form of fats, and twenty-five percent in proteins. In other words, at least half of your food intake should be in carbohydrate form. A few examples of common carbohydrates (which are made up of sugars and starches) are bread products, pastas (such as noodles, macaroni, and spaghetti), potatoes, vegetables, beans, fruits, cereals (such as wheat, rice, and oats), and sweets (such as hard candies, chocolate bars, and other high-sugar products such as raisins and dates).

Such strong emphasis is placed on a liberal carbohydrate intake for two reasons: First, sugars and starches enter the body's bloodstream almost instantly to provide quick energy for brief periods of required physical exertion. Second, carbohydrates also are quite easy to digest, which is important at elevations above 5,000 feet, where oxygen levels begin to diminish rapidly and rob the body of its ability to metabolize foods efficiently.

Fats also provide the body with energy, but since they are digested much more slowly they offer lower but sustained levels of go-power. Foods that contain high fat levels are dairy products such as milk, cheese, and butter. Nuts, egg yolks, and the marbling woven through the muscle fibers in beef also contain high levels of fat. (Most wildlife meats, by comparison, are quite lean.)

The third essential element, proteins, provides the body with minimal energy output over long periods of time. The primary roles of proteins in the diet are: production of body heat, maintenance of muscle tone, and the building and repair of cells and skin tissues. Common foods high in proteins include dairy products such as milk and cheeses, eggs, peanuts, cereal products, legumes such as peas and beans (particularly soybeans), and especially meat and fish.

It is interesting that 1 gram of fat liberates 9 calories of energy when burned, yet 1 gram each of protein or carbohydrate liberates only 4 calories. However, going back to what was said earlier, carbohydrates liberate energy almost instantly while the others do so over a longer period of time. The loss of 5 pounds of body weight is roughly equivalent to the burning of 15,000 calories. This explains why, in the face of strenuous exercise, such as mountain climbing, an individual may easily consume 5,000 or more calories per day and still lose weight during the course of a week.

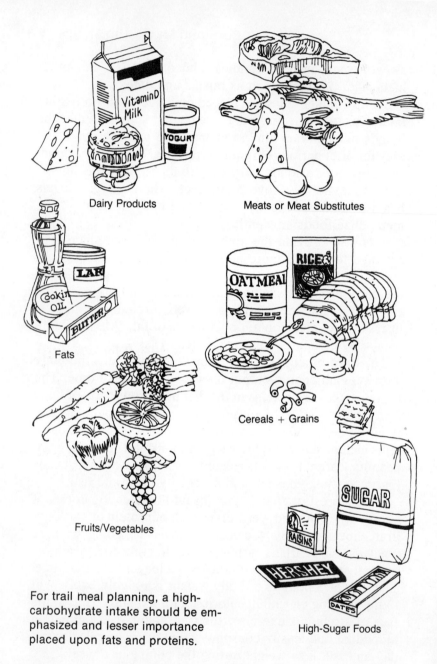

Dairy Products

Meats or Meat Substitutes

Fats

Cereals + Grains

Fruits/Vegetables

High-Sugar Foods

For trail meal planning, a high-carbohydrate intake should be emphasized and lesser importance placed upon fats and proteins.

Another way of looking at this, already touched on briefly, has to do with the complexity of the food molecules themselves. The most complicated ones (proteins and fats) virtually cannibalize themselves during the process of digestion. The digestion of food requires energy, with proteins and fats requiring the greatest energy. Fats may technically liberate more energy than carbohydrates, but less of the carbohydrates' fueling efficiency is lost during digestion.

This might lead you to believe that planning meals for a hunting, hiking, or fishing trip requires the expertise of a trained dietitian. Not so. Merely strive for a "balanced diet"—that is, one that each day on the trail adds up to a minimum of 3,500 to 4,000 calories, of which half are carbohydrates and the other half split equally between fats and proteins. Achieving this is easy if you include at least one generous helping per day from the following food groups: (1) dairy products; (2) meats or meat substitutes such as soybean products, nuts, cheeses, or eggs; (3) cereals and grains; (4) fruits and vegetables; (5) high-sugar foods; (6) fats, such as animal fat, butter, margarine, or saturated cooking oil.

To determine the actual grams and caloric values of foods in the above groups, consult reference charts found in detailed health-food guides. Better still, get a copy of the excellent *Agricultural Handbook, No. 8: Composition of Foods,* available for $2 from the Superintendent of Documents, U.S. Government Printing Office, Washington, D.C. 20402.

Then it is relatively easy to compile daily menus for outings of any duration that list not only total number of meals and specific items for each one but also the food-composition categories they fall into and the cumulative numbers of grams and calories those foods yield.

SAMPLE MENUS

When a lone hunter or angler takes to the trail, he already knows which foods he likes most and in minutes can piece together menus that offer sufficient caloric value and will satisfy his body's demand for carbohydrates, fats, and proteins. But when two or more outdoorsmen begin to plan meals, the debates that often ensue resemble an international summit meeting. One person loves meat and potatoes, while the other is partial to soups, stews, and fancy casseroles. Or one leans toward chocolate bars and "gorp," while another pleads for sourdough pancakes, biscuits, and bread. The only alternative is to compromise, which may be the most difficult aspect of a shared trail-cooking experience.

Aside from individual food preferences, the first order of business is to draw up a rough outline of the actual number of meals required for the duration of the outing. Consider a three-day weekend, for example, in which two hunters plan to leave home after breakfast on Friday morning and return in time for Sunday-evening dinner.

Friday	Saturday	Sunday
Trail snacks	Breakfast	Breakfast
Lunch	Trail snacks	Trail snacks
Trail snacks	Lunch	Lunch
Dinner	Trail snacks	Trail snacks
	Dinner	

A brief trek such as this one still requires seven sit-down meals prepared over a fire or some type of campstove. The "snacks" consist of assorted high-carbohydrate munchies (fully described in Chapter 4) prepared in advance to be eaten along the way as needed.

Next, it is necessary to fill in the menu more completely. Let's say the following breakdown evolves, after some negotiating.

	Serving size (ounces)	Grams of carbohydrates	Gms. proteins	Gms. fats	Total calories
Friday					
Snack					
Gorp	4	48	16	33	495
Lunch					
Chicken stew	11	23	21	6	223
Cheese, crackers	5	39	14	15	317
Fruit punch	8	30	—	—	120
Fudge brownies	4	43	6	27	412
Snack					
Jelly, crackers	2	50	7	2	230
Dinner					
Lasagna, sauce	11	41	18	8	315
Meat bar	3	—	41	35	478
Pilot bread	3	34	6	2	181
Lemon pie	7	63	3	2	280
Tea	8	—	—	—	—
Saturday					
Breakfast					
Western omelet	5	6	13	8	207
Sourdough biscuits	4	51	8	9	312
Bacon bar	3	3	30	30	400
Orange juice	8	33	1	1	147
Snack					
Banana chips	1	25	1	—	163
Beef jerky	1	—	16	4	100
Lunch					
Macaroni, cheese	12	54	15	8	344
Peas, carrots	4	9	1	—	44
Meat bar	3	—	40	35	450
Choc. pudding	5	31	5	1	148
Tea	8	—	—	—	—
Snack					
Trail brunch mix	3	53	5	11	330
Dinner					
Shrimp creole, rice	11	40	13	10	300
Green beans	2	3	1	1	27
Trail cookies	2	37	4	13	282
Choc. shake	9	54	12	2	273

(cont.)

	Serving size (ounces)	Grams of carbohydrates	Gms. proteins	Gms. fats	Total calories
Sunday					
Breakfast					
Pancakes, syrup	5	104	8	1	458
Sausage bar	3	3	30	30	420
Scrambled eggs	3	4	11	7	121
Coffee	8	–	–	–	–
Snack					
Apple chips	1	25	1	–	106
Peanut butter, crackers	2	42	16	9	309
Lunch					
Ham and cheese Romanoff	12	47	19	14	390
Fruit cocktail	5	35	–	–	145
Choc. nut cake	4	60	10	21	420
Lemon-lime drink	8	30	–	–	120
Snack					
Gorp	4	48	16	33	495

Let's assume the above menu, doubled in quantity to serve two individuals, will satisfy the palates of the hunting partners. If not, literally hundreds of other items (most of the above are standard freeze-dried or dehydrated foods available through any backpacking shop) could be substituted. I'll mention many of them in coming chapters.

In addition to offering exciting eating experiences, the above menu also allows for a minimum of 3,500 calories per person per day. And while proteins and fats have been included, a heavy emphasis has been placed on carbohydrate intake. This is especially the case with the mid-morning and mid-afternoon trail snacks, when the hunters are likely to need quick energy boosts to carry them up steep grades or, if they are lucky, to begin dragging a nice buck out of the hinterland. Outings of longer duration will require even more diligent planning to guarantee that each member of the party is continually supplied with adequate quantities of the right kinds of fuel.

When drafting menus either for brief or extended outings, however, give yourself some flexibility. Don't worry about possible food choices always adding up to specific daily calorie counts or an exact number of grams of carbohydrates compared to proteins and fats. The only instance in which these should be carefully monitored are during outdoor ramblings lasting more than two or three weeks. Besides, it is easy to supplement many types of dishes with an extra dollop of butter, a tablespoon of powdered milk (whole dry milk has more fat and therefore more calories than the low-fat or nonfat varieties), or whatever else may be needed to increase slightly the protein, fat, or carbohydrate levels of various meals. Bread or crackers can be spread with jam. And since tea and coffee are favorite drinks but contain no nutrients, they are easily fortified with a teaspoon of sugar or a squirt of honey from a plastic squeeze bottle.

Tip: Make a point of consuming perishable foods first, and those which are particularly heavy or burdensome second. Then begin working on the dry, lightweight mixes you've brought along that only need water to turn them into flavorful dishes.

CONSIDER THE SEASON

Certain times of the year or types of outings demand that adjustments be made in daily food requirements or options. A hunter or fisherman carrying a lightweight pack in summer and periodically having to push his carcass up steep grades may well get by with an intake of only 3,500 calories per day. Yet a late-season adventure seeker using snowshoes or cross-country skis, with the temperature not much above freezing, may burn as many as 5,000 calories. And those hardy souls engaged in mountaineering when it is less than 20°F may require 6,000 calories daily.

Cold weather places a tremendous strain on the body and stored-energy reserves because more than half the fuel consumed goes just to maintain body heat. The temptation often arises to slant the menu in favor of high-protein, heat-producing foods, but this can result in undesirable side effects. You might find you lack the short bursts of energy generated by the recommended 50 percent carbohydrate intake, or the sustained endurance levels produced by a daily regimen of 25 percent fat.

Rather than alter the food-group composition, it is almost always better to stick to the balanced diet and merely increase calorie intake as the temperature decreases. It's just a matter of eating more from each food group at each meal and, when on the move, consuming larger quantities of high-energy snack foods.

There is one notable exception. During cold weather, if you significantly increase your salt intake you'll stay warmer. This advice comes from Paul Petzold, the world-famous mountain climber, expedition leader, wilderness explorer, and founder of the National Outdoor Leadership School. According to Petzold's research, lack of salt tends to dehydrate the body and draw blood away from the extremities (arms and legs) toward the body's core, where the vital organs are, thereby increasing the chances of hypothermia or frostbite of the fingers, toes, and ears.

Conversely, additional salt intake keeps blood volume up and flowing to all parts of the body. This is why trappers and wilderness scouts of long ago relied heavily on bacon or salt pork as their primary meat staple, and during the winter months took large bags of salt with them into the backcountry. Fats (bacon bars, meat bars, buttered crackers) eaten just before retiring will also help you sleep warmer.

In warm weather, additional salt intake is important, not to help provide body heat, but to maintain a desirable electrolyte balance (see Chapters 3 and 7).

During torrid heat spells it's common to reach for a cold drink to cool off. Don't be surprised if you feel warmer, however: cold drinks require digestion, a by-product of which is energy, or heat. In other words, the more cold drinks you consume, the warmer you become. Conversely, warm drinks help you feel cooler. (Nutrition experts say the explanation of this would require an entire book, but try it and you'll see that small amounts of hot tea or coffee actually make you far more comfortable in hot weather.) When you crave a cold drink, though, orange juice rates top of the list, and of the lightweight, powdered varieties most compatible with trail tramping, Tang orange-juice crystals are far and away the most nutritious.

Seasonal-food choices. Sportsmen have an irresistible urge to leave gaps in menus, to be filled later with fish caught, game harvested, or wild foods gathered along the way. This is patently unwise because game can only be taken during certain months of the year and even then there is no guarantee the hunter's mark will be true. Fishing is not so critically influenced by the seasons, but fish themselves are notoriously fickle and can never be positively relied on to fill a pan. Wild foods, in terms of their presence, are not always available for the taking, either. Mushrooms and greens are predominantly products of the early spring and summer months, berries do not ripen until midsummer, and nuts seldom can be collected until fall.

By all means make use of any foods you may chance upon, but look upon them only as bonuses to supplement, or take the place of, meals already planned and brought along. If brookies are caught, glorious; save the freeze-dried beef stroganoff for another outing. But never leave the beef (or other main dinner entree) at home, confident the trout will be chewing the feathers off every fly in your pack.

2

Light Is
Right

It's incredible how much weight sportsmen have shed in the last twenty-five years. No, they haven't been adhering to strict diets — they're actually eating better than ever before — but it wasn't so long ago that a jaunt of a week or two into the wilds meant leading a string of packhorses loaded to the ears. Or using a 22-foot "freighter" canoe filled to the gunnels with 200 pounds of provisions. Today the same hunter, fisherman, or camper can easily make the same trek entirely on foot, stay twice as long if he chooses, and have all the needed essentials in a backpack that is not too heavy to tote seven miles per day.

To be sure, tents, sleeping bags, and other gear have undergone refinement so they are much more compact and lightweight than their predecessors. But pound for pound, the most significant revolution in outdoor recreation has been the boom in lightweight food technology. The same foods you enjoy in a restaurant have merely undergone freeze-drying, dehydration, and in some cases compression,

14

to result in backpackable products only a fraction of their original weights.

Drying food is the oldest known form of preservation. Hundreds of years ago Indians, nomads, and explorers learned that many foods, particularly fruits, vegetables, and meats, could be harvested, laid out in the sun to dry, and then stored without spoiling, to be eaten during the winter months when food supplies were less plentiful. Later they discovered that using various types of artificial heat dried the foods even more rapidly and effectively.

Tents, packs, sleeping bags, and cooking gear have undergone refinement and are lighter than ever before. But the most significant revolution has been the boom in lightweight food technology.

To this day, many farmers and rural families still dry foods in commercially available dehydration boxes that maintain precise temperature and humidity levels. On a much larger scale, major food processors worldwide have adopted both dehydration and freeze-drying techniques (just look at the dry packets of cheese found in casserole, noodle, and macaroni mixes in any grocery store). Or what about freeze-dried coffee, or the fruit in Post Raisin Bran? Milk, orange juice, meats, vegetables, potatoes, and soup mixes are other dried items commonly found on grocery shelves.

Dehydration is simply temperature-controlled drying in which up to eighty percent of a food's water slowly disappears by means of evaporation. But modern freeze-drying, called "vacuum sublimation" by scientists, is entirely different. This process sees fresh foods first flash-frozen and then placed in a vacuum chamber at about -50°F. Using this technique, the water originally contained in the food first becomes a solid (ice) but then changes to a gas (water vapor), which is sucked out of the chamber. When the processing is finished, the food is just slightly paler in color as before freeze-drying and slightly shriveled in appearance because ninety-eight percent of the water (which constitutes most of the weight of almost any food item) has been removed. Then the food is packaged in special oxygen-proof and moistureproof wrappers, which allow for an almost indefinite storage life.

In addition to freeze-drying foods, still another breakthrough in food processing was recently achieved by the Oregon Freeze Dry Foods Company (P.O. Box 1048, Albany, Oregon 97321). The new foods are called Space Savors, and the method of processing is called "compression." Using this technique, foods are first freeze-dried as described above, then subjected to tremendous amounts of

Comparative Chart of Wet and Dry Weights of Some Popular Freeze-Dried Foods

Product	Wet Weight (pounds)	Dry Weight
Strawberries	11	1
Cooked boneless chicken	3⅓	1
Green beans	14	1
Cooked shrimp	5	1
Mushrooms	14	1
Fresh pineapple	7	1
Cooked beef	3	1
Peas	5	1

pressure to reduce them to small discs. The idea brings us one step closer to the science-fiction tales of decades ago — that no one believed at the time — that one day in the future people would be able to eat several "pills" and receive all the vitamins, nutrients, and satisfaction otherwise derived from a hearty roast beef or turkey dinner with all the trimmings.

The main advantage of compressed foods is that a hunter or deep-woods fisherman can carry three to five times as much food in the same space ordinarily occupied by freeze-dried foods. Imagine 20 ounces of fresh green beans first freeze-dried and then compressed into a wafer weighing only 1.5 ounces, that after water is added will expand to original size, texture, and flavor and be sufficient to offer *five* ½-cup servings! Or a main course entree such as beef and rice with onions, originally weighing 1½ pounds, that can be carried in tablet form weighing only 5.4 ounces and then reconstituted to serve as dinner for two hungry mountain climbers.

Freeze-drying, then, reduces the weights of common foods by up to ninety percent; compression reduces storage space requirements by seventy-five to ninety percent.

Sun-drying of foods is the oldest method of preservation known
and is still highly effective.

Greatest achievement in food dehydration is modern freeze-drying
technique. Here, in vacuum chambers at the Oregon Freeze Dry
Foods company, vegetables and meats are first flash-frozen. After
the water in the food turns to ice it then is transformed into a gas
vapor, which next is sucked out of the chamber.

Freeze-drying reduces food's original weight by as much as 98 percent. Shriveled freeze-dried peas and carrots shown here retain their original color as well as their nutrients.

Lightweight foods originally were designed for cross-oceanic adventurers, mountain climbers, military personnel, and search-and-rescue teams, but they have long since been adopted by sportsmen who spend time in the wilderness.

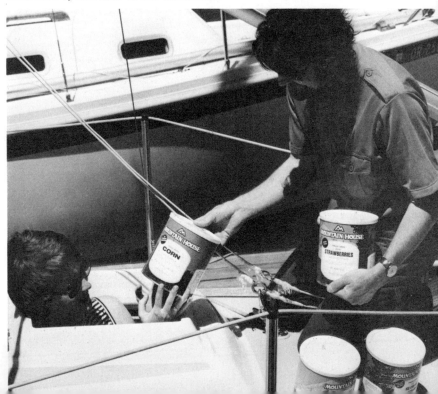

Ultimate in lightweight food technology is called "compression." Freeze-dried foods are squeezed into small discs to save weight and space.

All that is needed to reconstitute compressed foods is the addition of water. This tablet of green beans weighs only 1.5 ounces.

In a few minutes, the green beans literally explode back to their original size, weighing 20 ounces and offering five half-cup servings, yet none of the texture or flavor has been lost during the transformation.

SPECIAL BACKPACK FOODS

Of the several companies now preparing foods especially for campers, backpackers, hunters, anglers, and other breeds of outdoorsmen, the Oregon Freeze Dry Foods Company is by far the largest and most innovative. Long before the needs of sportsmen even were considered, the Oregon-based firm was fulfilling government contracts for nutritious, tasty, lightweight foods. More than 20 million field rations were shipped to Vietnam in the early 1970's. Before that, the company pioneered special foods for use in NASA's Apollo Space Missions, Sky Lab, and the confined quarters of the Defense Department's Polaris submarines. The special foods have also been adopted eagerly by Civil Defense groups, the Red Cross, Search and Rescue, and other government and private emergency-preparedness agencies.

In 1969 Oregon Freeze Dry Foods diversified and added a Mountain House Division to its corporation to cater to the needs of outdoor enthusiasts. The many foods made available subsequently contributed to the success of world-wide mountaineering expeditions to Mt. Everest, K2, McKinley, Annapurna, and many other famous peaks. They were also put to good use by racing sailboat teams and cross-oceanic adventurers. But their greatest popularity by far has been with average hunters and fishermen.

Just a few of the 102 food items presently available from Mountain House, in the meat category: pork chops, rib eye steaks, meatballs, bacon, and sausage. Main course entrees include noodles with chicken, chili with beef, beef stroganoff, spaghetti with meat sauce, lasagna with meat sauce, tuna á la neptune, shrimp creole, turkey tettrazini, beef almondine, and macaroni and cheese. Among breakfast items: several types of omelets, eggs, pancakes, and hashbrown potatoes. Vegetables include peas, beans, carrots,

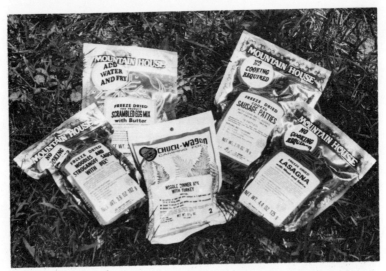

Several companies now make lightweight foods especially for out-doorsmen. Casseroles, meats, vegetables, breakfast foods, and desserts—requiring only the addition of water—are packaged in foil or plastic pouches.

corn, and mushrooms; fruits—apples, applesauce, banana chips, strawberries, pineapple, peaches, pears, and blueberries. Of the many desserts, the ones I like best are butterscotch-and-banana-cream pudding. Chocolate, vanilla, and strawberry ice cream—all freeze-dried—are also available.

In the special category of freeze-dried foods that come in compressed-disc form Mountain House offers three types of vegetables, two varieties of meats, and six main-course entrees.

The two next largest freeze-dried food companies are Chuck Wagon Foods, 780 N. Clinton Avenue, Trenton, N.J. 08638, and Rich Moor Corporation, P.O. Box 2728, Van Nuys, Calif. 91404.

One of the many Chuck Wagon complete-meal packets I regularly enjoy is labeled "Ranch Style." It consists of fancy oatmeal, milk, bacon-flavored scrambled-egg mix, cocoa, vegetable shortening, and the required mixing bags. Another of the company's popular complete-meal packets is a lunch called "Tuna Fish," which includes tuna spread, bolton biscuits, mixed fruit, chocolate-milkshake mix, gelatin dessert, and again the necessary plastic mixing bags. A favorite Rich Moor supper pack we have at least once on every outing includes tomato noodle soup, vegetable beef stew, dumplings, butterscotch pudding, and orange drink.

While a wide variety of these and other packaged trail foods can be purchased in camping, backpacking, and similar retail stores, they can also be ordered directly from the companies themselves. Merely request the company's catalog, then fill in the appropriate order form. There also are several mail-order firms that carry most of the well-known trail food brands along with other camping and outdoor cooking supplies. Two of the most recognized are Eastern Mountain Sports (EMS), Vose Farm Road, Peterborough, N.H. 03458, and Recreational Equipment Incorporated (REI), P.O. Box C-88125, Seattle, Washington 98188.

Deciding which trail-food company to buy from is largely a matter of individual preference. After a bit of experimentation and "field-tasting" you may decide you like one company's omelet better than another's. By the same token, you may find yourself preferring the tomato sauce in the noodle casserole made by one company to the cream sauce in the same kind of casserole made by another. Therefore the best bet, just as if you were shopping for food items to be prepared at home, is to try several brands over a period of time and let your palate be the final judge.

Using processed trail foods.   Many trail trampers prefer foods that do not have to be cooked. You merely open a pouch, add hot or cold water, allow the ingredients to reconstitute for five or ten minutes, and dig in. An added advantage to such foods is that they are prepared right in their own durable plastic bags, so there are no mixing bowls, pots, pans, or dishes to clean afterward. Just be sure to stir well after adding the water to thoroughly wet all the ingredients. Another thing I've learned by trial and error — mostly by error — is that if the product calls for hot water, it tastes much better if you use boiling water; conversely, if cold water is called for, the colder the better.

Other freeze-dried foods have to be cooked or simmered for variable amounts of time, most notably the compressed food discs by Mountain House but certain others as well. Some, unfortunately, need to be transferred to a small kettle of sorts, but many can be cooked right in their own plastic pouches. Generally, you open an outside foil packet, remove the plastic bag of food, submerge it in a pot of boiling water (don't cover the pot!) for five minutes, then eat solely or served over some type of pasta (spaghetti, noodles) or cereal (rice) dish.

As you've probably already many times noticed with conventional foods prepared at home, food-processing companies have a tendency to underrate the "hunger quotients" of active people. The same is true with freeze-dried backpack foods. Several times I've found a dinner labeled "serves four" could be gobbled up in short order by two hikers with many miles behind them at day's end. Keep this in mind when planning meals revolving exclusively around the use of commercial backpack foods. I vividly recall one of my first experiences with backpack foods, a six-day photo mission in search of elk in Wyoming's Grand Tetons. I planned meals for six days but found myself, after only two and a half days, totally without food and quickly scurrying back to civilization. Once my gear was packed in my trunk and I was on the road, my first stop was for gasoline and my second at the nearest steakhouse!

Another thing I've learned is that most processed foods can stand a great deal of improvement in the spice department. A bit of oregano or other Italian spices, blended herbs, poultry seasoning, or thyme sprinkled in will work wonders. Monosodium glutamate (MSG) as found in the brand name Accent is another distinct favorite. MSG has no flavor of its own but brings out the full flavors of other foods that may not be up to par due to the special processing they have undergone. (A nifty way of taking little samples of seasonings with you for only a few ounces of extra weight is described in the next chapter.)

I usually shy away from any freeze-dried foods requiring more than twelve minutes' cooking time but admittedly do make a special concession now and then on behalf of certain favorites. The only time no arbitration can be made is at the higher elevations where all meals, due to the lower boiling temperature of water, take a good deal longer. In this regard, when at elevations above 5,000 feet, be sure to read completely any special high-altitude cooking instructions printed on the packaging of various foods. Also, be sure to read Appendix 2, where high-altitude cooking and eating tips are discussed in detail.

There is one great drawback to highly specialized freeze-dried and compressed foods. Although most are very good (I didn't say "excellent"), outlandishly easy to prepare, and generally require minimum clean-up time, they are terribly expensive both in comparison to their grocery-store counterparts and in terms of what most sportsmen's budgets can comfortably afford. For example, one company's beef stroganoff dinner for two runs $5.60, compared to a name-brand supermarket variety for only $2.25 (these are 1981 prices). One company's backpack version of macaroni and

Special trail foods can be expensive. To cut the cost, buy large quantities at discount prices. Since the food has no expiration date, it keeps indefinitely and also provides reserves that may be needed for home emergency use.

cheese for two is $1.47; Kraft's version (to which you must add ¼ cup milk and ¼ cup margarine) is only 37¢. One company's freeze-dried spaghetti and meat sauce for two is $1.69; a dehydrated version available in any grocery store, 79¢.

So in many cases trail cooking can be terribly expensive. On the other hand, many may feel the higher prices are within reason in view of the foods' simplicity, light weight, and long life spans.

One way to significantly pare down the cost of eating freeze-dried foods in the outback is to buy them in large quantities. Most of the well-known backpack food companies readily oblige by offering a 10 to 15 percent discount on orders exceeding $100. Due to the extended shelf lives of these foods, there's the possibility of ordering several year's worth at one time (if you can spare the cash), storing them at home, and then using them as needed. This approach also provides an emergency food supply in the event of power failures, transportation strikes, and the like. However, if buying large quantities of trail foods is beyond your financial means, why not get together with several friends and submit a combination order?

SUPERMARKET FOOD CHOICES

A good way to have less expensive meals is to supplement freeze-dried trail foods with more economically priced items available at your local grocery store. The cardinal rule in doing this is to avoid the "keep refrigerated" labels; otherwise, the sky's the limit.

Small cans of stews, vegetables, meats, and casseroles are extremely handy. "Cans!" you exclaim. "Aren't they much too heavy for trail use?"

Well, I wouldn't want canned foods for outings of more than three days, but most people don't go longer than that anyway. Once or twice a year they may take off for a week or ten days, but there are numerous other ventures on weekends or during holidays that last only two or three days. This means planning no more than six or eight meals, so several items in small cans, tins, or plastic jars can easily be tolerated.

One distinct advantage of cans is that you need only remove the lids, set them directly on stove burners or around the fire, and allow their contents to bubble slowly to perfection in their own little cooking containers. No dishes are needed for these meals, either. Just grab a fork or spoon and go to it. For removing the hot cans from the stove or fire, get a lightweight handle especially designed for the task (some are included in cook kits) from your camping-supply dealer. Another handy item is a tiny G.I. can opener. It

Food in tins, cans, and plastic jars does have a rightful place in trail menus if the outing is brief and only a few meals have to be planned. Remember to pack out the containers when you leave.

Instead of taking a heavy can opener, use a G.I. opener that weighs only a half ounce.

weighs no more than a penny, costs about 25¢ and you get it in an army-surplus store.

Literally hundreds of dehydrated soups, beverages, side dishes, casserole mixes, and desserts line your grocer's shelves. In most cases the foods are freeze-dried or dehydrated the same way as those processed by the trail-food manufacturers. But since most of the supermarket varieties are not sealed first in plastic pouches, then again in foil heat-wraps to provide oxygen- and moisture-proof barriers, they carry significantly lower price tags. This simply means that the foods in your grocery store do not have the same infinite life spans as the specialized backpacking foods. But that poses little problem or worry for the person who merely wants food for an outing next week or next month.

A few words of advice on using supermarket foods for trail cooking, however: First, most of them are packaged in boxes that are too bulky to stow in knapsacks. So at home disassemble the packages and transfer their contents to sturdy plastic bags that have airtight closures, such as the popular Zip-Loc poly bags or those using twist ties. Cut the cooking instruction panel from the original box and place it in the bag with the ingredients, along with a slip of paper describing what the food actually is or any additional ingredients that have to be added (such as an egg, butter, milk, water). In many cases, the plastic bag you pack the food in can also be used as a mixing container.

Some of these foods truly are of gourmet quality. I especially like Kraft's new lineup of palate pleasers such as Beef Burgundy, Beef Stroganoff and Chicken Supreme. With these, and similar others, you heat a foil pouch in boiling water for five minutes, then pour the contents over noodles or rice to produce meals that actually are better than I can make myself from scratch. (Although no James Beard, I *am* an accomplished trail chef.)

To save weight and space, transfer the contents of packages to plastic bags. Remember to include the cooking directions from the box inside each bag.

Following are many foods I usually buy in supermarkets to supplement my specialized trail-food purchases, and browsing up and down the aisles yourself is sure to reveal countless others:

Breakfast Items

Pancake and biscuit mixes ("add water only" types)

Breakfast bars (highly nutritious; eat them as are)

Breakfast tarts (high in carbohydrates; heat over fire or stove)

Powdered eggs (mix with water or powdered milk and water)

Dried bacon bits (add to powdered-egg mix)

Dry cereals (add powdered milk, sugar at home; stir in water in camp)

Hash brown potatoes (add water, then fry in skillet)

Dried meats (eat as are, or soak in water five minutes, then fry)

Dried fruits (eat as are, or add to cereals)

Powdered-fruit juices ("add water only" types)

Cocoa (use "add water only" type; buy individual-serving packets)

Instant tea and coffee (use teabags; transfer coffee from glass jar to plastic bag or small plastic bottle)

Lunch Items

Assorted crackers (repackage to prevent breakage — see Chapter 3)

Peanut butter (repackage in plastic squeeze tube — see Chapter 3)

Jellies and jams ("nonperishable" types only — see Chapter 3)

Honey (buy, or repackage, in plastic squeeze tubes)

Instant soups ("add water only" types)

Bouillon cubes (excellent for soups and hot drinks)

Cheese ("nonperishable" types in squeeze tubes)

Tinned meats (sardines, oysters, clams, crab; all high in protein, fat)

Canned meats (salmon, tuna, vienna sausage, beef, chicken, ham)

Dry meats (ham, beef, chicken, salami, pastrami — buy in plastic bags)

(cont.)

Lunch Items (cont.)

Egyptian breads (very durable; store in moistureproof plastic bag)

Flavored noodle mixes ("add water only" types)

Flavored rice mixes (all Rice-a-Roni mixes are great)

Assorted cookies (chocolate cookies and fig bars offer high energy)

Canned puddings (Hunts brand is excellent)

Dry puddings (instant, "add water only" types)

Dried fruits (raisins, apricots, apples)

Instant beverages (presweetened lemonade, orange drink, Kool-Aid)

Dinner Items

Dry potato mixes (scalloped, O'Brien, au gratin, mashed)

Macaroni and cheese (repackage; add milk and butter later)

Spaghetti (repackage; use instant, "add water only" sauce mix)

Instant rice (add to soups, stews)

Noodles (add to soups, stews)

Bisquick (extemely versatile; use for pancakes, biscuits, frying fish)

Canned meats (drain away packing water, then fry)

Fresh meats (see Chapters 3, 12, 13)

Helper dinners (add canned meats, or dry meats soaked in water five min.)

Chinese foods (many varieties; meats and vegetables often in cans)

Casserole mixes (dehydrated beef stroganoff, tuna, turkey)

Dried vegetables (beans, peas, corn; add to soups, stews)

MAKING YOUR OWN

Drying one's own food for trail use is an enjoyable and rewarding way to spend a weekend or two, although not necessarily a way to save a lot of money. There are three ways to go about it: natural air drying; using a gas or electric oven in the kitchen; or investing in a commercially made home food dehydrator.

Those particular foods that lend themselves well to home drying include beef, venison, noncitric fruits such as apples, peaches, pears, prunes, apricots and grapes, and vegetables such as corn, beans, peas, carrots, onions, and peppers.

No matter which specific drying method is used, all foods should be in prime condition, and in the case of fruits and vegetables, ripe and just recently harvested. The essence of drying is to remove as much moisture as possible to prevent the growth of surface mold or the onset of bacterial spoilage from within. In accomplishing this, I've learned by trial and error that with natural air drying, where you live can be as important as any other factor. I happen to reside in southeastern Ohio where air drying is difficult if not totally impossible, due to our incessant mugginess and high humidity levels during all but the bitter-cold winter months. Therefore, it stands to reason other climates such as the desert southwest (Arizona, in particular), the windblown upper midwest states, portions of the midsouth (such as Kansas and Texas), and much of the Atlantic coast are far more conducive to air-drying foods than regions such as the rain forest of the northwest states or the semitropical environment of the Deep South.

To air-dry fruits, first remove their skins and trim away all inedible portions. Next remove stems, seeds, pits, or stones. (Prunes and apricots should additionally be scalded in boiling water for ten minutes.) Then cut into thin slices no more than 1/4 inch thick.

An inexpensive air-drying frame can be made from common fiberglass window screening stapled to 1"×2" furring strips. Set this tray outside, supported off the ground on sawhorses or wooden blocks of sorts so there is free air circulation beneath the screen, then lay your fruit slices on top. Finally, cover with a layer of cheesecloth to keep insects from landing on the fruit. The drying process should take anywhere from one to three days, depending on the temperature. It's wise to bring the entire screen assembly indoors at night, however. The fruit is dry and ready for packaging when it seems leathery and you cannot wring any water or juice out of it. I like to store it in Zip-Loc poly bags with as much air pressed out as possible. This fruit can be eaten in the dry state, used as is for cooking, or soaked in cold water before use.

To air-dry vegetables, it's wise to blanch them first to retain their natural color, texture, and flavor. After the vegetables have been cleaned, place small quantities at a time in a wire basket (such as the type you use for deep-frying fish or french fries) and immerse the basket into a pot of boiling water for about three minutes. Then quickly remove the basket and dump the vegetables into your sink filled with water made as cold as possible by the addition of ice cubes. Let them cool for about three minutes before removing.

Now, slice the vegetables thinly, or cube them if you prefer (as in the case of peppers or carrots), let them drain a bit on sheets of paper towels, then place them on your air-drying screen as you did the fruit slices. They will also take one to three days to dry, and are finished when they seem shriveled and hard (almost brittle). Store them in airtight containers and add them, as are, to soups or stews and let them slowly reconstitute by simmering. You can also soak them in cold water until they have regained their full size, then boil them for eight minutes in lightly salted water.

Oven drying of fruits, vegetables, and meats is accomplished in much the same way. Go through the usual preparation steps as previously described (with the meat, slice in ¼-inch-thick strips and remove every bit of fat and gristle). Larger pieces of fruit, vegetables, and meats can be placed directly on the oven racks, but small vegetables (such as corn, peas, or others that have been cubed) will have to be placed on cookie sheets. Place the food in the oven, set the temperature dial at about 140°F, leave the door slightly ajar, and the food should be dry in a number of hours. Then, store as usual in airtight jars, transferring the contents to plastic bags as needed for trail use. (For full details on making "jerky," see page 59.)

Those who are successful with these drying methods may wish to get more fully involved by purchasing a commercially made home food dehydrator. Prices run from $50 to $300, depending mainly upon the number of shelves and other features included. Basically, such units are rectangular cabinets that stand on end, with the food shelves or trays pulling out like drawers. All of the ones I have seen are electrically operated, fan-blown affairs that allow precise control of temperature and humidity levels.

The Garden Way Company, Charlotte, Vermont 05445, offers several different types of home food dehydrators, as does the Laacke & Joys Company, Milwaukee, Wisconsin 53202 (see Appendix 1). Also, the magazine *Mother Earth News* frequently has advertisements on behalf of companies that sell home food-drying equipment, in addition to occasionally running articles describing how to make various types of dehydrators in home workshops.

There also are countless other types of foods and meals anyone can prepare in advance at home. The kitchen cupboard is sure to yield dry ingredients that can be plastic-bagged and require only the addition of water later or perhaps a small tin of meat. Blended soups are a splendid example. Or homemade macaroni and cheese (use only dry, powdered cheese). Cold or hot breakfast cereals also can easily be made by premixing the cereal, powdered milk, sugar, and pieces of dried fruit in a plastic bag. At breakfast time, merely stir in hot or cold water. By using instant potatoes, noodles, rice, dried meats, dried vegetables, and spices, you can prefabricate stews and casseroles. The list of other possible ideas is limited only by your imagination and willingness to experiment.

Just remember in all cases to label each plastic bag so you know what's inside, the serving size, and the specific wet ingredients that must later be added. Then, use a felt-tipped pen to identify the proper sequence of the meals in your trip menu, such as "Breakfast, Day 2," "Lunch, Day 3," and so on. This way, you stick closely to your menu—and to proper nutritional requirements and a balanced diet.

In coming chapters I'll be describing many meals that can be economically prepackaged at home to supplement freeze-dried, dehydrated, or other commercially available foods. To kick things off, here are several favorites I rely on for many outings.

Tuna and Noodles

4 oz. enriched egg noodles
2 oz. dehydrated peas and carrots
1 envelope dry chicken-noodle-soup mix
1 6½-ounce can white tuna

Mix the dry ingredients in a plastic bag, then slip in the can of tuna (unopened, of course). In camp, place the dry ingredients in a small kettle, add 2½ cups very hot water, and slowly simmer until the noodles are almost soft (about 8 minutes). Then add the tuna, cover the pan, and simmer an additional 5 minutes. This meal feeds two hungry people and is especially good served over piping hot biscuits.

Tomato Rice with Beef

1 ½ cups instant (Minute) rice
1 envelope dry tomato flakes (or dry spaghetti-sauce mix)
1 tablespoon dry onion flakes
1 6 ½-ounce tin of beef, or one 4-ounce bag of dry meat
½ teaspoon salt
¼ teaspoon black pepper

Mix the dry ingredients in a plastic bag. In camp, bring 1¾ cups water to a boil in a small pot. Add the dry ingredients and stir well. Then add the beef and stir again. Cover the pan, remove from the heat, and let sit for approximately 5 minutes or until the rice is fluffy and the meat hot. Serves two.

Hearty Chicken Soup

2 oz. dehydrated stew vegetables
2 chicken bouillon cubes
1 6-oz. tin boneless chicken or one 4-oz. bag dry chicken
4 oz. dry, wide noodles
¼ teaspoon salt

At home, place the noodles in one plastic bag and the remaining dry ingredients in another. In camp, bring four cups of water to a boil, add the noodles, and slowly simmer until they are almost cooked (about 8 minutes). Thoroughly crumble the bouillon cubes, then stir in. Add remaining ingredients, cover the pan, and let slowly simmer 10 minutes. Serves two.

Fancy Oatmeal

1 cup dry oatmeal
$\frac{1}{2}$ cup dry powdered milk
$\frac{1}{4}$ cup raisins
$\frac{1}{4}$ cup brown sugar

At home, place the dry ingredients in separate plastic bags contained in one larger bag. In camp, cook oatmeal per instructions on box (either clip them off box or write them on a slip of paper and include in the bag). When the oatmeal is done, stir the dry-milk powder into 1 cup hot water until dissolved, then add to the oatmeal along with the raisins and brown sugar. Continue to stir over low heat until everything is hot. Serves two.

3

How to Tote the Toughies

By the time my friend Wayne Parker was only twenty-two, he had already received three proposals of marriage. He turned them all down, however, insisting that when the right time and right woman came along, he would do the asking. Eventually the right woman did appear, and Parker, an ardent sportsman, decided to learn firsthand if she felt the same way about the outdoors as he did. After they had become well acquainted, he suggested they go on a back-packing trip to a beautifully remote lake nestled in a pine-studded rimrock somewhere in Montana's Glacier National Park.

Fortunately, Mary, a novice to this sort of thing, did take an immense liking to backpacking. This meant, in Parker's mind, that the time was right. He waited until dinner and, with a bed of glowing coals ready, pulled two absolutely prime T-bone steaks out of his pack and in seconds had them sizzling on a wire grill. He reached into his duffle a second time and retrieved a cool bottle of inviting Cabernet Sauvignon, along with a corkscrew and two crystal wine glasses.

If you've guessed Wayne Parker popped the question soon after the wine bottle's cork, you're right. And Mary answered with a hearty "yes."

This true story proves that backpacking does not necessarily have to mean "roughing it." Depending on the time of year and length of the journey, enterprising sportsmen can easily partake of food and drink on the trail that few others would ever consider.

Consider, for instance, how Wayne Parker was able to serve steak and wine prior to his wilderness proposal. To begin with, the time element was conducive to the meal. It was only a two-day outing, and therefore required only five meals. Since the total walking distance (going in and coming out) was only 8 miles, carrying the weight of the steak and wine, along with four other meals consisting of lightweight backpack foods, was no hardship.

Due to the brief nature of the trip, packaging and preserving the meat was no problem, either. The steaks were frozen in advance at home, wrapped tightly in aluminum foil, then wrapped again in several layers of newspaper. Indeed, when Wayne and Mary unwrapped the steaks eighteen hours later, they discovered the meat had not yet entirely defrosted. The wine and crystal glasses also were packed in newspaper (crumpled), then secured in Wayne's sleeping bag. (Naturally, the empty bottle was carried out afterward.)

Other meats—pork chops, chicken, bacon, sausage, ham, seafood, hamburger—will also travel far down the trail in good shape. Just remember that meats must first be frozen solidly and then wrapped securely; the outing must be brief so the meats don't have a chance to defrost thoroughly and begin to spoil; the other foods for the remaining meals should be lightweight and compact so the weight of the fresh meats does not become a burden.

On outings of three days or longer, fresh meats can still be used if they are worked into the menu as some of the first

Meats should be solidly frozen, wrapped in foil, then wrapped a second time in newspaper. Depending upon the air temperature, meats wrapped this way may remain frozen for up to two days.

foods consumed. Cold weather — nature's refrigerator — also helps preserve meats during long periods. Transporting them is easy if there are several members of the party willing to shoulder the added weight.

LIQUIDS

Aside from meats, liquids can be troublesome because of their weight and tendency to leak if improper containers are used. Water is the primary liquid most hikers have to carry (see Chapter 7). Two others are cooking oil and syrup (if you prefer not to use the dehydrated, add-water-only type — one item made by trail food manufacturers that tastes lousy). For either of these, I heartily recommend any of the special plastic bottles made for 'packers. The many sizes and shapes are a matter of individual preference, but rectangular ones with wide mouths are easiest to pack and use. These bottles range in size from ½ ounce to 1½ quarts, and cost anywhere from 25¢ to slightly more than $1.

Two tips about buying bottles: First, be sure to get only one that specifies "positive locking, no-leak cap." Usually it has a special gasket that fits between the rim of the bottle and the cap, or a plug that is inserted into the mouth of the bottle before the cap is screwed on. Second, only buy those bottles made of odorless polyethylene.

Another liquid many like to have along is a bit of Old Scalplifter for end-of-the-day socializing while poking the fire. Again, select one of the many plastic (never glass) bottles or flasks made for backpacking use, but be careful to avoid the few labeled "not suitable for alcohol." You can also use a kidney-shaped bota, or wineskin.

Botas are ideal for transporting many types of beverages. They are designed to conform to the body's contours, so they are not uncomfortable to use like some canteens. And since you use a bota by holding it up high and squirting a thin stream of liquid into your mouth, it's a fun way to make limited quantities of water or other beverages last longer. The best botas are made of leather lined with a tasteless, clear latex that can be removed for easy cleaning.

In addition to drinking water in a canteen or plastic bottle, I like to hike with a bota filled with Gookinaid ERG, Husky Aid or Gatorade. All three are sold in specialized backpacking shops, and through many camping mail-order catalogs. The Gatorade is also commonly found in grocery stores. These drink mixes come in powdered form and need only the addition of water, so you can take liberal yet

Plastic bottles are lightweight and handy for transporting liquids, syrups, and similar items. They come in numerous shapes and sizes, and those designed for backpacking will withstand almost any kind of rough treatment.

A soft wineskin, or *bota,* is ideal for many types of beverages.

Be sure bottles have special no-leak caps. Some varieties feature a gasket under the lid; the author favors those with an insert plug (shown here).

lightweight quantities on outings and replenish your supply as you go along. Although originally designed for athletes, these beverages are ideal for outdoorsmen because they not only quench thirst more efficiently than other beverages, but their ingredients are designed to replace the electrolytes (dissolved salts) passed off in great quantities through perspiration during strenuous exercise. If these salts are not replaced, a hiker is far more prone to fatigue and muscle cramps, particularly at the end of the day when the air temperature begins to drop. And, believe me, simultaneously getting a charley horse in each leg, while trapped inside a mummy-type sleeping bag, will have one doing a St. Vitus dance more quickly than hobbling over a bed of hot coals. Yet now and then taking a healthy swig of Gook, Gator, or Husk usually prevents cramps or that tail-dragging feeling that often comes at day's end. Of the three beverages, Gookinaid ERG (*E*lectrolyte *R*eplacement with *G*lucose) is probably the most recognized by medical authorities for maintaining body-salt balance while decreasing the danger of fatigue, heat exhaustion, and dehydration. I pack a large envelope for every outing, and at the beginning of each day add about two teaspoons to my water canteen or bota.

Another popular potion among active sportsmen is Thermotabs, a brand of nonprescriptive tablets containing sodium, potassium, calcium, and dextrose. When engaging in very strenuous exercise I take one tablet five times a day and never notice heat exhaustion, cramps, or that wiped-out feeling at day's end.

EGGS AND OTHER FRAGILE FOODS

Fresh eggs, like meats, can be taken on brief outings. This will come as good news if you have a strong dislike for powdered eggs, as many do.

There are many tried and proven methods of transporting eggs on the trail. One approach, if you're having pancakes

Special high-impact egg cartons offered by camping-supply outlets serve dual purposes. In addition to protecting eggs from breakage, they can later be used to pack out nonburnable foil and other trash. The author's son Mike holds a dozen-egg carton. Others are available for transporting fewer eggs.

for the same breakfast, is merely to wrap each egg separately in a small plastic sandwich bag and then bury all of the eggs in your bag of pancake flour. This way they are buffered and protected from breakage, but if an egg does break, it is saved and not allowed to contaminate the flour. Or, at home, crack as many eggs as you'll need and dump them into one of the wide-mouth plastic bottles described earlier. If you're careful in handling such bottles the egg yolks will remain intact; otherwise, you'll have to learn to like scrambled eggs. There are also durable plastic egg cartons available through camping supply dealers; they hold either six or one dozen of the "cacklefruits." When the eggs are gone, use the handy carton to stow nonburnable foil and other refuse that must be packed out.

Whatever the decision, take to the trail only with eggs that are as cold as possible (but not frozen) and plan to use them as soon as possible. They'll keep longer if you first dip each egg in hot paraffin to give it a sealed covering (eggs are very porous and the thin layer of wax prevents air from entering and causing spoilage). Eggs that have a hydrogen-sulfide odor when cracked are spoiled and should not be eaten; if there is no hydrogen-sulfide odor, the eggs are safe to eat.

Crackers are also quite fragile, and the big cardboard boxes they come in, much too bulky for trail use. I generally transfer the crackers to a 4″×3″ plastic freezer container with a moistureproof snap-top lid. One container will amply serve two hungry hikers at lunchtime (along with cheeses, meat spreads or other foods). And, here again, once the goodies are consumed, you have a tightly closed receptacle for housing trash temporarily.

Bread products are susceptible to being crushed, squashed, or torn. They are also quite vulnerable to moisture. Use plastic freezer containers for these, too. Or stick with items such as Rye Krisp, Pilot Bread, Egyptian Bread, Mt. Logan Bread, or Bolton Biscuits, which are more sturdy and easier to store and transport. Egyptian Bread and Rye Krisp should be available in your local grocery store; the others are sold by backpacking outlets that carry foodstuffs.

One important reminder about packing virtually any type of food is that the foods to be used during the final days of the outing should be located near the bottom of the knapsack, while the first to be consumed should be near the top. This saves having to dig through all kinds of bags and containers to locate a particular item when it's needed. Also, be sure the foods are somewhat centered in the pack, with padding (such as clothes) surrounding them. This is critical because underbrush, sharp rocks, tree limbs, and other obstacles along the side of the trail can sometimes puncture or

Crackers are very high in carbohydrates and excellent with meat or cheese spreads as high-energy snacks. To prevent breakage, stow them in a lightweight plastic freezer container, then later use the box to store and pack out nonburnable trash.

Crackers and breads also are made by backpack-food companies. Bolton Biscuits and Pilot Bread are very sturdy and come packed in moistureproof cellophane wraps.

tear plastic or foil food bags inside the pack even though there is no visible evidence of damage to the exterior of the pack.

BUTTER AND CHEESES

Margarine is extremely high in fat content — in fact, it's the most concentrated energy food available — and therefore affords sustained levels of endurance over long periods of time.

Many people mistakenly assume margarine requires refrigeration because that is generally how they buy it. It will indeed last longer that way and even can be frozen for long-term storage. But it's quite common to go into a grocery store in a tiny village far back in Canada's wilderness, for example, where electricity is costly and in short supply, and find boxes of margarine stacked right on the shelves along with canned goods and other nonperishables.

If you're skeptical, simply read the package and see if there is a "keep refrigerated" label. Among the nonperishable brands, which most are, the all-vegetable margarines will keep better than those which contain milk solids. Butter is an excellent substitute for margarine (I much prefer it to oleo), but since it is made from cream it requires refrigeration and can only be used during cold-weather outings.

I like to let margarine (or butter) sit at room temperature until it is soft and then transfer it to a plastic squeeze tube.

The type of tube I prefer is available through camping supply dealers, and looks like a large, clear toothpaste tube with a screw cap at one end and a removable clip at the other. The clip allows the entire back end of the tube to be opened and any type of soft food inserted. The end is then folded over about ¼ inch, and the clip put back in place. To use, just unscrew the cap and squeeze.

These tubes are also great for peanut butter, vegetable shortening (if you'll be making breads or pies in camp), honey, pancake syrup, cheese spreads, mayonnaise (in cold weather), and nonperishable jellies and jams. All of these items are high in the three essential food elements and are invaluable to every conceivable type of trail cooking.

Cheeses can be taken on most treks into the backcountry. Cheddar keeps best, but others will remain in good condition without refrigeration for many weeks if they are packed properly. I'm talking here about *real* cheeses, not processed spreads that really are only cheese-flavored milk solids and are highly perishable.

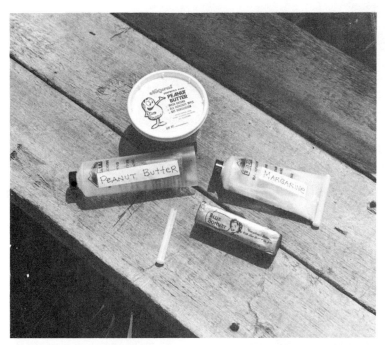

For transporting soft foods such as margarine, peanut butter, jam, syrup, or honey, use special plastic tubes made for this purpose. Removing a clip allows food to be inserted in wide back end of tube; later, just squeeze it out other end like toothpaste.

The way to package cheese is to first remove it from its foil or cellophane wrapper and rewrap in several layers of cheesecloth pressed firmly into the cheese on all sides. Then, tie a short string to a corner of the cheesecloth and dunk the cheese into a pan of melted paraffin to give the works a tight coating. Each time you want a slice of cheese to eat or use in cooking, carefully peel back a corner of the paraffin-soaked cloth, remove what you need, then tightly fold back the cheesecloth. If a bit of surface mold (harmless penicillin) appears after several days, pay it no mind. Just slice it off with your knife before eating.

Spices, condiments, seasonings, and similar items should be transferred from their larger containers to 35mm film canisters, to save weight and space. Label each container.

Instead of taking large, heavy containers of salt, pepper, or other spices and food additives, use the tiny packets you get in fast-food restaurants or with carry-out orders.

When traveling ultralight, even coffee and salad dressing can be obtained in lightweight packet form. Stow a wide assortment of these items in your food bag and let campers help themselves.

Dry spices, condiments, and seasonings (sugar, salt, pepper, baking soda, Italian seasoning, poultry seasoning, chili powder, and others) are easily stowed in plastic 35 mm film canisters with moistureproof snap-top lids. Be sure to use indelible ink to label the outside of each can. Keep all the cans together in a lightweight cloth or plastic bag.

Get in the habit of saving the little complimentary packets of spices and other goodies so readily available these days. You get them with meals on airplanes, trains, in restaurants (especially the carry-out fast-food places)—almost anywhere food is served. In my travels I accumulate paper packets of salt, pepper, and sugar, as well as plastic or foil envelopes of salad dressing, mustard, ketchup, instant tea, instant coffee, nondairy creamer, tartar sauce, honey, and lemon juice. In many restaurants, at breakfast time, you're likely also to be given little tubs of margarine, maple syrup, and nonperishable jellies and jams. All of these are extremely convenient for trail eating because they come in individual-serving portions. This eliminates the added weight of larger containers holding excess quantities you probably won't be able to make good use of during the outing.

Stow an assortment in a plastic bag or nylon sack that you can bring out at each meal, and let everyone help himself. When traveling ultralight, simply slip several of the ones you're certain you'll need into their appropriate meal bags.

▲▲ 4 ▲▲▲▲▲▲▲▲▲▲▲▲▲▲▲▲▲▲▲▲▲

High-Energy Snack Foods

Physicians and nutritionists who work with professional athletes spend awesome amounts of time formulating special diets that allow for an increase in calorie consumption that matches the athletes' increased levels of physical exertion. Since muscle tone is so crucially important to football and baseball stars, it stands to reason a high percentage of that calorie intake is in the form of protein. Fats are of next importance, for sustained levels of rigorous endurance, with carbohydrates invariably receiving the lesser priority of the three. A ready example of this regimen is the dining room of any training camp, where platter after platter of thick steaks adorn long tables. Yet one has to search long and hard to find the mashed potatoes and gravy or the lemon-meringue pie.

Sportsmen are influenced by different circumstances, however. Muscle tone is important, as is the ability to maintain sustained levels of endurance. But much higher on the list of requisites are short bursts of energy between meals, during brief periods of strenuous exertion. As we saw earlier, carbohydrates fill this need because sugars and starches, due to their easy digestibility, enter the body's mainstream almost instantaneously.

A trail tramper who knows what he's doing, then, begins nibbling on high-carbohydrate snacks only minutes after the breakfast dishes are cleaned and he's off in search of fish or game. And he continues this eating all the way through the day until bedtime, pausing at suitable times for lunch and dinner.

Such eating habits, it might seem, would fill you up like a balloon. That would indeed be the case were you back in the city working at some sedentary activity in an office. But on the trail, an outdoorsman continually burns large quantities of energy and periodically needs extra go-power. An ongoing refueling process is crucial.

I usually begin this energy intake the minute I begin walking by sucking on a hard candy in my mouth. These are almost pure sugar, and I keep a wide assortment of different flavors in my pocket in order to vary the routine. If I suddenly anticipate a long, steep haul, I'll further boost my energy level by eating a candy bar.

If the trail is not so demanding, or I'm casting lures to fish or leisurely evaluating the terrain for fresh game signs, I like to munch occasionally on other goodies, such as the dried banana chips made by the Rich-Moor Trail Food Company, the sliced pears and apples (freeze dried) made by Mountain House, and Chuck Wagon's strawberry tear-sheet.

These and still others are special trail snacks specially made for outdoor types. But in your local supermarket you'll discover many other lightweight, highly nutritious foods than can easily be adapted to trail use. I'm thinking, for one, of granola bars, or the endless variety of dried fruits, and especially the candies (your kids can show you exactly where these are). Look also for the handy bags of

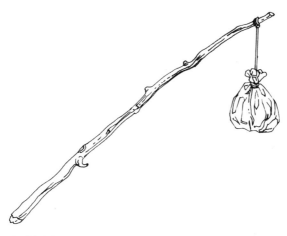

Popcorn is highly nutritious and lightweight, and "hobo popcorn" is a special treat for kids because they can easily make it themselves while sitting around the evening campfire.

sunflower kernels, toasted pumpkin seeds, and the many types of Nature Snacks being produced by the Sun-Maid Raisin Company.

One snack that goes over well with kids is Hobo Popcorn. Popcorn is high in carbohydrates and fats for extra energy and when eaten just before retiring will help you sleep warmer. It's a special treat in the evening especially if kids have registered a bit of displeasure with the Beef Wellington or other "fancy food" Mom and Dad may have enjoyed for dinner. What the kids like perhaps even more is that they can make the popcorn themselves.

Spread out a 14-inch square of heavy-duty aluminum foil for each child on the outing. Now, press the foil into your cupped palm with your fist and pour in 2 tablespoons of popcorn and 1½ tablespoons of cooking oil. Next, bring the corners of the foil pouch up and twist them, so you have a baglike affair. At the twist, tie an 8-inch length of string, then tie the other end to a long stick (the type you might use to roast hot dogs). When sitting around the campfire at night, each kid can dangle his Hobo Popcorn bag over the coals (not too closely or it will burn) and give it a gentle shake now and then. As the corn pops it will expand the foil bag. When it stops popping the corn is done and it can be eaten right from its own container by merely peeling back the foil.

A little popcorn goes a long way, and it's fairly lightweight. I store mine in a plastic sandwich bag closed with a twist-tie.

GORP: THE ALL-DAY LUNCH

Trail-food manufacturers have given it their own names: Power Snack, Birdseed, Trail Brunch, Squirrel Food, Nutrimix, Energy, or Lurps. But whatever the brand or the particular blend of ingredients, sportsmen, campers, and backpackers the world over simply call it "gorp."

Gorp actually is an acronym for "*g*ood *o*ld *r*eliable *p*eanuts," although some stalwartly disagree, claiming gorp means "*g*ood *o*ld *r*aisins and *p*eanuts." Whatever the case, it's indication enough of the main staples in this high-energy trail food. A lightweight trail snack you can buy from any backpacking food company, or make at home yourself, gorp is absolutely packed with very high levels of carbohydrates, fats, and proteins. A 1½-ounce serving of Lurps, made by Mountain House Foods, provides 6 grams of protein, 15 grams of fat, and 20 grams of carbohydrate, to produce a whopping 250 calories of quick energy. The ingredients consist of chocolate bits, cashews, peanuts, and freeze-dried raisins.

Another brand I like (available in grocery stores) is called Power Snack by the Woodfield Farms Company. A 1-ounce serving provides 5 grams of protein, 8 grams of fat,

Backpack-food companies give it their own names, but trail trampers universally call it "gorp." The favorite snack of all backpackers, it consists mainly of peanuts, raisins, seeds, candy, and dried fruit. Gorp is very high in carbohydrates for instant energy needs.

Carbohydrates are invaluable to outdoor people because they enter the body's mainstream almost instantly. With a high-carb snack, you're a bite away from quick energy.

and 13 grams of carbohydrate, for an instant energy output of 129 calories. The ingredients are dry-roasted peanuts, raw cashews, raw pumpkin kernels, raw sunflower kernels, and raisins.

Since special backpack foods are comparatively expensive, however, many people prefer to make their own gorp at home. There are only two important things to keep in mind: At least fifty percent of the gorp mix should consist of peanuts, while the remaining fifty percent can be a random assortment of candy, fruit, seeds, or whatever; second, the various items must be of a nonperishable nature.

One extremely popular gorp recipe, invented by Steve Netherby, an expert backpacker and California-based camping writer, is made up of the following:

---

1 large bag of peanut M&M's
1 large bag of chocolate M&M's
1 medium-size box of raisins
1 1-pound can of salted sunflower seeds
1 1-pound can of salted peanuts
1 10-ounce can of salted mixed nuts

This recipe is nothing short of delicious, but variations sometimes see the substitution of chocolate or carob drops for the regular M&M's, chopped dates for the raisins, or the inclusion of soybean seeds or dried apricots. Experiment to determine what you like best.

Plan on a minimum of 8 ounces of gorp for each day on the trail. I like to mix up a large batch, then stow daily allotments in small plastic sandwich bags closed with twist ties. After breakfast, just before breaking camp, I take a new bag out of my pack and put it in an exterior pocket of the pack (or my jacket) where it will be handy.

Many sportsmen prefer to make their own gorp. You'll need about 8 ounces for each day on the trail. Store it in a plastic bag with a zip closure.

MAKING JERKY

Jerky dates back hundreds of years and probably is the most widely known trail food. Since it is extremely high in protein, early trappers and pioneers heavily relied upon it during the winter months to produce body heat quickly.

In simple terms, jerky amounts to little more than dried meat. Since the meat is dehydrated, it is very lightweight and requires no preservation. The dehydration process removes approximately eighty percent of the meat's water, so it's easy to see that 10 pounds of raw meat is necessary to produce a quantity of finished jerky weighing only 2 pounds.

Early settlers used the venison of deer, elk, moose, caribou, and sometimes even bear meat or buffalo to make jerky. Modern adventurers can use any of these, too, if they are available, but when they are not, lean beef will do. I like to use round steak, but other cuts are suitable as long as they are about ½ inch thick and relatively free of fat; any existing fat should be trimmed completely away.

Begin by slicing the meat into strips that are ½ inch wide by 6 inches long. Always slice with the grain, rather than against it. Place one layer of the sliced strips in the bottom of a glass bowl and then lightly sprinkle the meat with a flavored salt of your own choosing. We prefer hickory-smoked salt, but onion or garlic salt is also fine. Then add another layer of sliced beef strips and repeat the salting process. Add as many layers of meat as the bowl will hold, then cover and place in your refrigerator overnight. This will allow sufficient time for the meat to become pleasantly seasoned.

The following day place the strips of beef on an ungreased cookie sheet and pop the entire works into an oven. Or, skewer toothpicks through the ends of the strips of meat and suspend them, so they hang vertically, from the oven's wire racks. Another popular recipe eliminates the seasoned salt and calls for brushing the meat strips with Liquid Smoke before placing them in the oven.

You don't want to cook the meat, just dehydrate it, so set the oven temperature at about 180° F and leave the door slightly ajar. The drying process will take approximately five hours.

When finished, the jerky will have a coal-black appearance, but the meat is neither burned nor charred. It should seem rather tough and leathery to chew, with no moisture left in it. If you find the meat is still moist in the middle, let it dry another hour.

At home, we store our jerky in a wide-mouth glass jar with a loose fitting screw-cap lid. For trail use, we put what we need in individual plastic sandwich bags closed with twist-ties or string.

In addition to being a very tasty and nutritious snack, jerky also can serve as the meat in many types of meals. Simply break a number of jerky sticks into bite-size pieces and add them to soups, stews, or casseroles. The jerky will

To make jerky, first slice lean meat with the grain. Use venison or beef, and be sure all the fat is trimmed away.

Next, add the strips of meat to a glass bowl and flavor with hickory-smoked salt or any seasoning of your choice. Then cover bowl and place overnight in refrigerator.

The next day, skewer the strips of meat with toothpicks and hang them in your oven. The idea is not to cook the meat, only dehydrate it, so set the oven's temperature dial at about 160° to 180° and let the jerky dry for four to six hours.

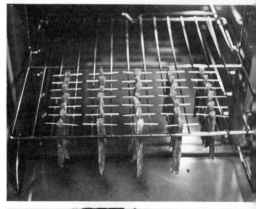

The finished jerky is coal black but not burned. It doesn't require refrigeration. At home, store it in a wide-mouth glass jar with loose-fitting lid. For trail use, transfer to a plastic bag.

quickly absorb moisture, the same way freeze-dried foods rehydrate, and swell up in size to become tender meat again.

PEMMICAN: THE INDIAN TREAT

It's a little-known fact that North American Indians harbored virtually insatiable sweet tooths. These were satisfied by a meat "dessert" called pemmican until white traders came along with cinnamon sticks and peppermint. During their travels, Indians also relied upon pemmican to fill a nutritional void that otherwise would have presented itself through a strict diet of jerky alone.

The earliest recipe I can find for original Indian pemmican saw deer or buffalo meat first dried under the sun and then pulverized. Next, crushed berries and nuts were kneaded with the meat, and the resulting "mash" put into membranous pouches made from animal intestines. Finally, bear grease was rendered and poured into the pouch until it began to leach out through the pores. The pouch, once the fat cooled and solidified, was called *pimikin*. It was then buried deep in the ground where it would remain cool, and cached at locations along commonly used travel routes, to be used when other food sources were scarce.

Modern sportsmen who take to the trail like pemmican as well. Not only is it tasty and versatile, but highly nutritious, as well. To be sure, few of us have ready access to buffalo meat, animal intestines, or rendered bear fat. But a facsimile of the original pemmican can easily be made at home for use later in the backcountry.

Take 2 pounds of venison or lean beef, slice it into strips the same as in making jerky, then steam the meat in a double boiler until it is thoroughly cooked. Next, run it through a meat grinder.

Then, through the grinder also run 1 cup each of dried peaches, dried apples, chopped peanuts, and blueberries. (Feel free to vary this recipe by substituting dry prunes, blackberries, or other fruits or berries.)

Next it's necessary to bind all the ingredients together. Some prefer to knead the ingredients with 1 cup of melted beef or venison fat (that has had a chance to cool slightly), or vegetable shortening. Others like to use a mixture of ½ cup each of honey, margarine, and peanut butter.

Finally, make "candy bars" out of the pemmican, put them in plastic bags, and store in your freezer until you are ready for an outing.

You can munch on pemmican like candy, fry it in a pan with sliced potatoes, add chunks of it to stews or soups, or cut very thin slices to be eaten with bolton biscuits during lunch.

Because of the berries in the recipe, plan to consume your pemmican within two days after removing it from your home freezer, unless the outside air temperature is below 40° F.

5

Wild Edible Plants

I'll never forget the time I met the late, famous Euell Gibbons, author of *Stalking the Wild Asparagus* and one of the world's foremost experts on wild edibles. It was in Columbus, Ohio, at a nature seminar where numerous authorities were on hand to provide outdoor writers with information pertaining to wild foods. What I remember most occurred at noon when there was an intermission for a buffet lunch and we casually began ambling into an adjacent room where long tables were stacked with platters of roast beef, barbecued chicken — the works.

As it happened, Euell decided to "eat out" that particular afternoon. If you think he went across the street to grab a burger and 'fries, you're mistaken. He did go across the street, but to a vacant lot seemingly festering with overgrown weeds. *That* was where our hero enjoyed his noontime meal, nibbling at this, picking at that, his eyes lighting up with each new find. I do not remember the specific items on Gibbons' menu that day, but I do recall his saying later that he had eaten nine different plants of more than two-dozen edible ones he had located.

The point Euell Gibbons wanted to make this day soon became clear: In North America there are about 20,000 classified plants, of which 2,000 are known to be edible. If a man can find twenty-four of those in less than one-half hour on a vacant lot in the heart of a major city, imagine what he might chance upon during the course of several days hiking through fields and forests!

As emphasized at the beginning of this book, sportsmen should never abbreviate their planned menus in hopes of finding wild foods or harvesting fish or game. But wild plants and greens are everywhere, and when edible ones are discovered they can add an exciting, flavorful tang to any meal. Although most wild plants are relatively low in fats and proteins, some are very high in carbohydrates and nearly all are high in natural vitamins and minerals.

IDENTIFYING POPULAR EDIBLE PLANTS

Identifying certain edible plants and greens is accomplished by carefully examining the shapes of their leaves, stems, stalks, buds or flowers, the coloration of all of these, and the plant's conformation (the size and placement of various parts of the plant in relation to each other). In time, it becomes possible to recognize wild edibles at a glance, as easily as you know the onions, carrots, and lettuce in your home vegetable garden.

The following wild edibles are commonly found in most parts of the country. Since they are easy to identify and very flavorful, they are the unanimous favorites among trail trampers.

Arrowhead (sometimes called duck potato, tule potato, wapatoo, or wapato). This is an aquatic plant found growing in the shallows of marshes, ponds, and along the shorelines of lakes and slow-moving rivers. Slender green stems from 6 to 36 inches tall support green leaves shaped like arrowheads that are 2 to 9 inches long and half as wide. The leaves are parallel-veined and may be floating on the water or standing just above the surface on their stalks. Small clusters of white flowers may be present. The edible part of the arrowhead plant is the tubers, which are about the size of large radishes and look very much like potatoes. They grow as part of the root system, in the mud or sand, at the base of the plant. You can knock the tubers loose with a stick, or kick them free with your feet, and they will float to the surface for easy retrieval. Arrowhead tubers can be cooked the same way you would new potatoes, but taste even better. Boil them and serve with butter, fry them, or slice and add to soups or stews.

Burdock   (sometimes called burr weed, gobo, or beggar's buttons). Burdock is commonly found along roadsides, hiking paths, fence rows, field edges, and particularly around abandoned buildings such as old log cabins or deserted structures around farms and sawmill camps. The plant is not easily mistaken because of its numerous thistle-like burrs that adorn the stems and are notorious for clinging to the garments of those who brush against them. Burdock plants often stand 3 to 6 feet tall. From a main, green stalk grow side stems holding most of the leaves and burrs. The leaves are roughly heart-shaped and when young are quite smooth to the touch. White or purple flowers may be present; underneath them are tendrils that readily attach themselves to clothing. All parts of the plant except the flowers and burrs are edible. The roots of young plants can be peeled, sliced, and simmered for 15 minutes in water to which ¼ teaspoon baking soda has been added. After the allotted cooking time, discard the water, cover again with fresh water, then continue boiling until the roots are tender. Early in the year the leaves, stems, and stalk can also be eaten. Peel the stems and stalk, slice, add to a pot of water, and bring to a boil. Then discard the water, add fresh water and now the leaves, bring to a boil again, and cook until tender. Serve with melted butter the same way you would spinach or broccoli.

Cattail.   This aquatic plant is unmistakable. It most frequently can be seen in clusters fringing the shorelines of ponds and lakes, and is also found in swamps. Long, slender, grasslike leaves grow up from the base of the plant. From the center grow several long, fibrous stalks with the familiar brown autumn "spikes" perched on the ends. Cattails usually grow 3 to 6 feet high. At the base of the plant, just below where the leaves separate, is a white, round shoot. It smells and tastes very much like cucumber and can be eaten raw or sliced and added to salads. Cattail roots have a durable, leathery skin that when peeled away reveals a white core that can be prepared any way you would potatoes. Inventive cooks can also roast the roots, grind them, sift the resulting "meal" from the remaining stringy fibers, and use it in place of flour to make biscuits or hotcakes.

Dandelion. Anyone who cannot recognize the dandelion undoubtedly spent his entire childhood years cloistered indoors. The plant is so terribly common in lawns and yards that most green thumbs look upon it as a nuisance. Yet dandelions are higher in vitamin A than any other plant on earth. They thrive in open fields, grassy meadows, and along overgrown logging roads and hiking trails. The only time dandelions may be difficult to find is late in the season when competing vegetation has grown high, as there is the tendency for the dandelion's lion-tooth leaves to lay flat on the ground. Look closely, however, and the plant's telltale yellow flowers may reveal their locations. The leaves can be eaten anytime of year, but they are most tender very early in the spring. Later, they may have a somewhat bitter taste, which can be removed by boiling twice in fresh pots of water. Serve the same as broccoli or spinach, or eat the young leaves raw in a salad. The roots of the dandelion plant can also be used to make an excellent beverage that closely resembles coffee. Peel the roots, chop them, then roast until hard and brown. Use 1 teaspoon of root bits per cup of coffee; bring water, with roots in it, to a boil and let it slowly simmer for 5 minutes; strain out and discard the roots before drinking.

Dock   (sometimes known as curly dock, sheep sorrel, wild spinach, or numerous other "dock" names). Dock plants are widely abundant and easy to recognize. From slender, stout stalks grow alternating stems, each developing into a long, dark-green leaf that somewhat resembles a narrow spearhead. Generally the leaves are from 2 inches to 2 feet in length and have wavy or curly edges. Near the top of the plant, which may be several feet tall, are tiny stems bearing seeds which appear green early in the year, then turn brown in fall. Although these seeds can be dried, ground, and used

as flour or meal, what most backwoods folks really relish are the green leaves. They have a faint lemon flavor when eaten raw and are excellent in salads with just a bit of oil and salt. When cooked in boiling water until tender, they taste very much like asparagus.

Lamb's-quarter (sometimes called pigweed, goosefoot, or wild spinach). Many consider dock and lamb's-quarter the two best of all the wild greens, and both were distinct favorites with early settlers and pioneers. Lamb's-quarter plants grow from 1 to 6 feet tall and have a special fondness for popping up where the soil has been disturbed. Meadows, previously plowed fields, power-line right-of-ways, old logging roads, fence rows, game trails, and along the edges of

hiking trails are fine places to keep an eye out for lamb's-quarter. The plants themselves have single, slender stalks with alternating double-stems that end in leaves that are roughly diamond- or egg-shaped but with edges serrated with broad teeth. The leaves usually are dark green on top, light grayish-green underneath, with a vague, floury-white cast all over. By the end of summer a lamb's-quarter stalk will yield enormous clusters of tiny seeds (sometimes as many as 75,000 per plant). Outdoorsmen can eat the entire plant when it is young; boil the stems, leaves, and stalk in water for several minutes until tender, or eat the various parts raw in a salad. (When the plant grows older and larger it is better just to eat the small, new leaves.) The seeds can be dried, ground into meal, and used to make hotcakes. They can also be boiled until soft and eaten as a hot breakfast cereal.

Watercress (sometimes known as pepperleaf). Watercress is an aquatic plant that thrives in cold, moving water and can be found in the same types of places where trout live. With roots buried in the bottom, the stalk grows upward and the resulting leaves usually lay matted and wavering in the current near the surface. Flowers are present during the warmer months, and they resemble four-leaf clovers but are white in color. Although the stems of watercress plants can be eaten, most people prefer only the leaves; they are roughly heart-shaped, dark green in color, segmented, and smooth to the touch except for their wavy edges. Boil the leaves briefly (until they are tender), or add them to raw salads.

Wild lettuce (sometimes called chicory weed, chicory lettuce, or horseweed). Wild lettuce is not only eagerly sought by human gatherers of wild greens but is also a favorite with many wildlife species, such as deer, small game, and upland birds. It is even liked by domestic-livestock species—hence the nickname "horseweed." Wild-lettuce plants closely resemble dandelions because their leaves are similar. However, the wild-lettuce plant sprouts from ten to twenty yellow flowers, and the plant stalk often grows 6 feet high. The leaves are long, narrow, with deeply serrated fingers extending from the main vein, and the bases of the leaves are tightly wrapped around the main stalk. The leaves are shiny green on top with a whitish-green color underneath. If you break the stalk, you'll find a milky juice inside. Small wild-lettuce plants are excellent raw in salads. Strip the leaves from the main stalk of older, taller plants and boil until tender.

Preparing wild greens. Generally, wild greens are most tender and flavorful when they are very young and eaten raw, while older and larger plants are better cooked. Also, cooked plants are better when served singly as you would vegetables such as broccoli or asparagus, while young plants eaten raw in salads are usually better mixed with several other varieties.

If there's a good chance I'll come upon greens along the trail, I prepare salad dressing in advance and pack it in a small plastic bottle. An easy dressing to make consists of 1 part vinegar to 3 parts salad oil. Or use any of the handy salad-dressing packets mentioned earlier that are available in restaurants and fast-food joints.

Another salad-dressing recipe that not only tastes good but is perfect for counteracting the slightly bitter flavor of certain plants such as mature dandelions is the following:

---

4 tablespoons vinegar
10 tablespoons salad oil
2 tablespoons mayonnaise
$1/4$ teaspoon salt
$1/4$ teaspoon pepper

Be careful with the mayonnaise in this recipe; it's highly perishable.

Melted bacon fat also makes a good salad dressing. Dribble several tablespoons over a mixed salad, then toss briefly.

Many types of greens can be added to soups, stews, and casseroles, but it is difficult to make them taste any better than when served *au natural*—unless, perhaps, when a generous dollop of butter or margarine is stirred in.

6

Nuts, Berries, Fruits, and Roots

It is exciting to read adventure tales of early North American heritage and how colonists and settlers pioneered the wilderness by placing great reliance upon the killing of game for sustenance. But it is likely many of the writers who chronicled those early times were more romantic than realistic, because diaries and trading-company logbooks preserved in historical archives tell a slightly different story. They reveal that before agrarian lifestyles began to predominate—around the middle of the nineteenth century —our forefathers did indeed regularly hunt, but they were also diligent gatherers of food growing about them. They recognized the nutritional values of wild greens, nuts, berries, and fruits. Moreover, they quickly learned from Indians that when hungry they could far more consistently rely on gathering such food, rather than the chancy prospects of stalking a deer or catching smaller game in a snare.

Much of the "new territory" was densely forested and given a wet spring, the following autumn was certain to see woodland floors carpeted with walnuts, hickories, chestnuts and butternuts—all free for the taking. Naturally, where trees existed there also were roots, which could be made into beverages or used for medicinal purposes. And where small clearings for homesteads began to appear, sunlight penetrated the forest canopy to foster the growth of berries and fruits.

Of course, most modern trailblazers do not need to rely on these wild foods in the nutritional sense, nor to fill carbohydrate, fat, or protein needs. Still, there are not many serious outdoorsmen who will choose to overlook such prized finds when they happen upon them. Aside from the health benefits of wild foods, most edible nuts, berries, fruits, and beverages made from roots are just plain good eating. And the fact that they are gathered from fields and forests in exactly the same manner as pioneers did hundreds of years ago makes any outdoor adventure all the more meaningful.

IDENTIFYING COMMON NUTS

Nuts are high in proteins and fats and so delicious that at least three wild varieties—black walnuts, pecans, and pinyon pine nuts—are harvested commercially. (So was the native American chestnut until an Asian blight destroyed nearly all of these stately trees in the 1920s and 1930s.) In any regard, nuts drop off parent branches in the fall months when they have matured. The ones you're most likely to find on the ground in forested regions are easily identified.

Black walnut. The native range of the black walnut stretches from Massachusetts to Minnesota and southward to the higher ground of the Gulf states. The tree has dark, uniform bark, and the leaves and nuts are unmistakable. The leaves are of the compound type in which a single stem

1 to 2 feet long gives birth to eleven to twenty-three "leaflets" 2 to 5 inches long that grow opposite each other along the central axis. The nuts are enclosed in spherical green husks about 1½ or 2 inches in diameter, and they hang singly or in clusters of twos and threes. These green husks, when broken apart to obtain the roughly ridged nut inside, will leave a harmless but temporary brown stain on your fingers. The meat of the walnut is sumptuous, but the shell is thick and hard; you'll need a rock to break it apart, and then perhaps the tip of your pocketknife blade to pry out the nutmeat. It's worth the effort, however, because then the meats can be eaten raw as you pick your way along the trail. For a special treat, save a few meats to add to pancake batter, or sprinkle them over hot breakfast cereals.

Butternut. Butternut trees are found in all states east of the Rockies, but they prefer temperate climates. Look for them in rich woods, on open slopes, and along old logging roads and fire trails. The bark of the butternut is deeply grooved and brownish gray in color. Like the black walnut, the butternut's leaves are compound, growing opposite each other along a central stem. The stem averages 15 to 30 inches long and possesses seven to seventeen leaflets from 2 to 4½ inches long. Butternuts are oblong, or football-shaped, and 1½ to 2 inches long. Their grooved, rough shells are encased in green, wrinkled husks. The nuts are delicious mixed with "gorp."

Hickory nut. There are many species of hickory trees, but the shagbark hickory produces the finest eating nuts. Shagbarks are plentiful from Maine to North Dakota and south to the Gulf Coast. The tree is easy to identify because of its ragged plates of gray bark which curl away from the trunk at the edges. Here again is a tree with compound leaves, but the distinguishing feature of the hickory, in addition to its unusual bark, is the presence of only five leaflets. The nuts are contained inside greenish-yellow husks 2 to 2½ inches in diameter. These husks break away rather easily, but, underneath, the shells holding the nutmeats are quite hard to crack. You'll need to pound on them with a rock and employ a good many expletives to salvage them. The nuts, once retrieved, are best eaten raw, added to cold cereals, or used as a garnish in wild green salads.

Pecan nut. Pecans are actually the largest of the hickory-tree species. It is not unusual to find them in the wilds growing to heights of 160 feet, with 4-foot-diameter trunks. They are primarily trees of the warmer, southern climates but have been transplanted far beyond their original Mississippi Basin range. The leaves are compound, averaging 9 to 20 inches in length, with nine to fifteen leaflets, 3 to 4 inches long. The nuts, shaped like footballs, are 1 to 2 inches in length, and contained in brown outer husks which peel away easily. These nuts grow in clusters of three to eleven, and the shells are usually thin and easy to break. Mix pecans into any of your high-energy snack foods, eat them raw, or break them into bits and sprinkle over desserts such as canned puddings.

Pinyon-pine nut. The pinyon pine is a native of the higher elevations west of the Rockies but has been transplanted elsewhere. You'll find it in mountainous country at 5,000 to 10,000 feet altitude. Generally the pinyon pine is a small bushlike tree with green needles only an inch long that grow in bundles of twos and threes. Technically, pinyon nuts are

really only small seeds discarded by the lumpy-looking pine cones, which average 2 inches in diameter and are sphere shaped. Munch on the seeds the same as you would sunflower or pumpkin seeds.

BERRIES AND FRUITS

There is cause for rejoicing when berries or fruits are randomly discovered along the trail, and a special event indeed when a large find is within brief hiking distance of camp. Most berries popular among "pickers" come to maturity in mid to late summer, while fruits usually are products of the cooler fall months. Play it safe and eat only those you can positively identify. There are more than 160 different species of edible berries and wild fruits. These are the ones I like best and find most often:

Blackberry. No one who spends much time outdoors should have trouble finding or identifying this favorite. Blackberries are rarely found in deep woodland areas but thrive along trails, old logging roads, in burns and clearcuts, on open hillsides, or almost anywhere else the terrain is exposed to ample sunlight. As in the case of all berries, some years there are bumper crops and other times seemingly none at all. When there are few to be found, the culprit almost always is a late spring frost that "burned" the immature flowering buds of the berry bushes. Blackberries grow in shrublike fashion, seldom exceeding 6 feet in height. Ragged-looking 1- to 2-inch-long green leaves, thin stems that break easily, thorns that love to prick exploring fingers, and fruits that are tiny and red in spring and gradually enlarge and turn black by July are the hallmarks of blackberry bushes. As many as fifty berries may adorn each stem, and prized finds are berries called "thumbers," mean-

ing they are as large as one's thumbnail. Enjoy them raw, with milk and sugar, sprinkled over your breakfast cereal, mixed into pancake batter, or dig out your reflector oven and make a pie!

Chokecherry. Chokecherries grow all the way from South America north to the Artic Ocean, and they are popular with outdoorsmen because they have a unique way of quenching one's thirst. The cherries grow on large shrubs, thereby distinguishing themselves from most other fruits, which grow on trees. Chokecherry leaves are egg-shaped, 1 to 4 inches long, abruptly pointed at their ends, and with numerous serrations along their edges. The cherries, about

¼ inch in diameter, may be either black or dark red, and there are often dozens on each stem, causing the branches to droop low to the ground. Each cherry has a pit, or stone, which is poisonous and should *not* be eaten, but the pulpy fruits are slightly tart and delicious. Eat them raw or use them as a topping on otherwise bland cereals such as oatmeal.

Currants. More than seventy-five varieties of currants grow coast to coast, and are often referred to as "gooseberries." They generally grow on shrubs or bushes with stalks adorned by greenery that looks much like maple leaves. Some currants are wine colored but the most popular species, which average ½ to ¾ inch in diameter and are pale green with darker green stripes, causing them to look much like miniature melons. Like chokecherries, currants slake one's thirst when eaten raw, but they also can be cooked and then used as a fruity jam on crackers, or made into pies.

Elderberry. Elderberries grow on shrubs that range from 4 to 12 or more feet tall. They are found coast to coast but thrive in damp soil. Leaves of the elderberry bush are lance shaped, 1 to 3 inches long, sharp at the tips, and with ragged edges. The berries, averaging ¼ inch in diameter, grow in enormous numbers on thin stems that branch and rebranch. Mature elderberries are red and quite bitter tasting compared to the more desirable black or blue ones. Many do not care for elderberries eaten raw (I do) but prefer them cooked and added to pancakes, muffins or hot cereals.

Pawpaw.   The pawpaw is a large shrub or small tree with purple flowers in spring and large leaves that often droop over. The leaves may be as much as 8 inches long; they are narrow at their stem attachments, widen quickly to several inches, then abruptly become narrow again to end in sharp tips. The species thrives east of the Mississippi wherever there are shaded areas with damp soil. A prime place to find pawpaws is along stream bottoms deep in forest glens, along the shorelines of lakes or on adjacent hillsides. The fruit of the pawpaw averages 4 inches in length and looks like a stubby banana. Immature pawpaws are green; mature ones, bronze or golden brown. Almost the instant pawpaws come to maturity they fall to the ground; hence, a hiker must be on hand at just the right time to gather them before they spoil. If they are yellowish brown on top but black underneath, they have been lying too long. The fruit, best eaten raw, has a sweet custardlike substance inside that is almost certain to please even the most discriminating tastebuds.

Persimmon. The native range of the persimmon tree stretches from Pennsylvania to Iowa and south to the Gulf states. The bark of the tree appears like individual plates, or corrugations, almost like alligator hide. The species grows most frequently along the edges of open fields where there are fence rows or stone walls. The leaves of the persimmon tree are 3 to 7 inches long and resemble smooth, shiny lance heads. The persimmons themselves often remain on their parent twigs long after the leaves have fallen, and it may be necessary to use a long stick to knock them free. The fruit usually is less than 2 inches in diameter, smooth, round, and slightly orange in color. The best eating persimmons are those which have reached maturity after the first hard frost in fall. I like to eat them raw.

Wild black cherry (sometimes known as rum cherry). Wild black-cherry trees flourish in all states east of the Rockies. They can be found in moist, rich soil as well as dry barrens where few other trees exist. The bark of the wild

cherry closely resembles that of the shagbark hickory, with irregular plates and thick scales that curl up around the edges. Also look for horizontal white lines on the bark that serve as "breathing pores." The leaves of the wild black cherry are lance shaped with serrated edges, 1 to 4 inches long, and sharp at their tips. The fruit, averaging ¼ inch in diameter, grows in clusters on long stems and is not mature until early fall when it turns dark purple or black. Wild black cherries are excellent eaten raw, added to cereals, or included in your favorite muffin mix.

SASSAFRAS TEA AND WILD COFFEE

I remember my childhood days in Cuyahoga Falls, Ohio, and a place called Reuther Field near our home where my pals and I congregated at least once a week to play baseball. My brother Jeff, a budding naturalist at the age of only eight, often tired quickly of standing in the outfield where he customarily was stationed and soon could be seen exploring for bugs, snakes, or unusual plants. It was from him that I learned about sassafras and the sumptuous tea that could be made from it. Dozens of times we'd trod home from a game clutching our bats and mitts in one hand, several of the saplings in the other, and quickly engaged Mom's help in preparing the tantalizing brew. To this day, I still gather sassafras on my farm and game preserve in southern Ohio, or whenever I'm traipsing around elsewhere in search of fish or game.

Sassafras. Sassafras trees are found east of the Mississippi, from the Gulf states north to Canada's fifty-third parallel. The trees thrive in open fields or along trails and logging roads where they receive long periods of direct sunlight. There are two extremely easy methods of identify-

ing sassafras. First, the smooth-edged leaves, averaging 2 to 6 inches in length, are shaped like mittens with either one, two, or three fingers (called "lobes"). Many times all varieties of the leaves are found on the same tree. If in doubt about the species, however, pull up a small sapling about 3 feet tall, sniff the roots, and you'll detect the distinct, very pleasant aroma of root beer. Don't worry about killing an occasional sassafras sapling for tea. The species grows in such thick groves, it soon crowds itself to such an extent that the trees become stunted and sometimes even die. The best thing any stand of sassafras can have happen to it is a bit of periodic thinning. Scrub the roots clean in cold water, scrape them with the blade of your pocketknife to remove the outside skin, then chop them into pieces and add to a kettle of boiling water. Slowly simmer for about ten minutes, and watch the tea turn a rich amber color. Some like to add milk and sugar; most prefer it straight.

Wild coffee. The wild-coffee plant has the same distribution as sassafras (east of the Mississippi, from the Gulf states north into Canada). It is also found on hillsides and in thickets exposed to long periods of sunlight. A central green stem is covered with tiny hairs and grows to 5 feet tall; opposing leaves line each side of the stalk. The leaves are football shaped, with smooth edges. At the bases of the leaves, where they are attached to the stem, are small bell-shaped flowers, underneath which are brownish-orange berries that average ½ inch in diameter and ripen in late summer and early fall. These berries can be dried, roasted, and ground to make a coffee beverage that is difficult to distinguish from the store-bought variety. Use a pot of cold water and add 1 heaping teaspoon of wild-coffee grounds for each cup of coffee, bring to a boil, remove from the heat source, and allow the brew to steep for five minutes.

7

Indispensable Water

Outdoor ramblings put a lot of things in their proper perspective. You discover muscles you didn't know you had and become reacquainted with what fresh, clean air really smells like.

You also learn the value of numerous things you otherwise take for granted, like clean water and the enormous quantities we use—and waste—during the course of a normal day at home. For example, you're dry as a biscuit from mowing the lawn, go inside, turn on the faucet, then nonchalantly begin searching around in the cupboard for a glass. Meanwhile, two quarts of clear, cold stuff have vanished down the drain. Or, you flush the john and there go seven gallons of water. *Seven* gallons!

But so what? Well, as I said, the outdoor world is a far different existence from metropolitan life, and there was one time I would have given a couple of sawbucks, maybe more, for a mere pint of precious clean water. This was in Colorado, in the White River National Forest, while I was trailing a mule deer buck. It was a torrid October—an unseasonable 85 degrees—but my 2 quart canteen was half full so without good sense I pressed on through the ovenlike heat. Now and then I took a swig.

Eventually dusk fell and I decided to establish a lightweight lean-to camp, eat dinner, grab some shut-eye, then take after the buck again at daylight.

Suddenly, the jolt of reality struck. I began to feel dehydrated but barely a sip of water was left in my canteen. There was not enough even to begin to slake my thirst, let alone prepare the freeze-dried spaghetti dinner in my pack, or the powdered eggs and orange juice I had brought along for breakfast the next morning, or to clean any utensils afterward. It was too dark to begin stumbling around in search of a stream, spring seepage, or rock cavern where water might have collected.

To tell the truth, I felt like a first-class idiot. I also spent one of the most hellacious nights of my life sucking on a pebble in an attempt to keep my mouth moist and my mind off something to drink. The following morning I was parched beyond description and even beginning to feel a bit punchy. As soon as it was light enough to see my boots, I gave up the hunt and with due haste hightailed it back to civilization. It took two full days of nursing untold gallons of liquids before I was my real self again. Had I continued after that buck there's no telling where my bleached bones might now be lying.

One thing I obtained on that hunt, if not venison, was a valuable lesson: Water is a vital commodity to outdoor folks. It is priceless compared to the raft of gadgets that sometimes bulge our pockets, like a Swiss Army Knife, for instance, with its leather punch, scissors, sewing awl, and thirteen other accessories. Water is even more important than any food that might be in your pack, because survival experts say you can easily go three weeks without eating but in hot weather only seventy-two hours without replacing lost body fluids.

Exactly how much water a sportsman needs depends, as we have just seen, upon the weather, but also the length of the journey, the degree of strenuous activity involved, and the types of meals on the menu. Therefore, personal experience often is the best teacher. But let's pin it down a little more than that.

In hot weather, while engaging in moderately strenuous hiking and other exercise, figure you'll need to drink 1 gallon of fluids per day. This may be strictly water or a combination of water, fruit juices, Gatorade, coffee, and so on. Then add another gallon for preparing meals, cleaning cooking utensils, and in the evening enjoying a spartan sponge bath to remove some of the trail grime. Altogether, that's 2 gallons per day.

In cooler temperatures you can get by with only 2 quarts of fluid intake per day, but still will probably require the same extra gallon for meal preparation, clean-up, and the like.

Now, consider that water weighs 8 pounds, 5 ounces per gallon, and you're looking at a minimal requirement of about 12 pounds of water per day during the most congenial weather conditions. On a three-day trek, then, that amounts to 25 pounds of water or more to serve various purposes. It doesn't take a whiz kid to tell us that is a prohibitive amount of weight to stash in one's pack along with food, clothing, tent, sleeping bag, and other gear.

The best compromise is always to carry at least 2 quarts of water with you and plan to obtain the remainder, as needed, along the way.

A variety of acceptable containers will transport the 2-quart minimum. In hot weather I like a blanket-covered canteen that I keep slung over my shoulder like a bandolier. The water supply is always handy this way. And at night, I hang the canteen from a tree branch, soak down the blanket covering, and the combination of night breezes (even

My favorite water containers include (from left to right) blanket-covered 2-quart canteen, aluminum 1-quart model, plastic 1-quart Army surplus canteen, and plastic quart bottle.

though warm) and evaporation will have significantly cooled the water so it is more refreshing the following day on the trail. If I expect to do a lot of perspiring, I also like to have along a bota filled with 1 quart of Husky Aid, Gookinaid ERG, or Gatorade to replace lost electrolytes and hopefully eliminate leg and shoulder cramps.

In cool weather, I often have along the same bota but now a 1-quart belt canteen of durable plastic, which is much lighter than the blanket-covered shoulder model. Another 1-quart plastic bottle rides in my pack.

In cold weather—you guessed it—the bota is with me again (I absolutely loathe charley horses). But now my minimum 2-quart water supply is carried in a brace of leakproof plastic bottles stashed inside my pack where they will not freeze.

FINDING WATER ALONG THE WAY

Planning water requirements for an outing is just as crucial as planning the menu, and it's wise to rely upon the knowledge of someone who is familiar with the lay of the land. Ask a rancher, for example, about the locations of springs on his property, rock crevices where water trickles down from higher elevations, or other sources, and carefully mark the exact locations of each on your map. Ask, as well, about the water in streams, rivers, or lakes you are likely to come across, which of them are too contaminated to draw water from, and which would be suitable if purification methods were used.

In the case of public lands, check in advance with the local game warden, forester, or BIA (Bureau of Indian Affairs) agent. Or stop by the local office of the U.S. Forest Service, Agricultural Extension Agency, State Department of Natural Resources, Bureau of Land Management (BLM), or Soil Conservation Service (SCS). You're sure to find someone who knows the terrain you'll be exploring and can advise you about the availability of water.

Then, whether hunting, fishing, or just camping, you should be able to plan each day's travel in such a way that rest breaks and evening camps coincide with locations where you can conveniently replenish your water supply.

Lakes and rivers are almost sure to be where people tell you to look for them, or where they are indicated on topographical maps. This isn't true with other water sources. Streams, springs, and seepages have a nasty and unpredictable way of suddenly disappearing. Or, you may arrive at a year-around spring, or perhaps even a lake, sadly to discover the water has become stagnant, brackish, foul smelling, contaminated by livestock or wildlife, or for some other reason is not drinkable. In this event, it is invaluable to be able to know how to find water other ways in other places.

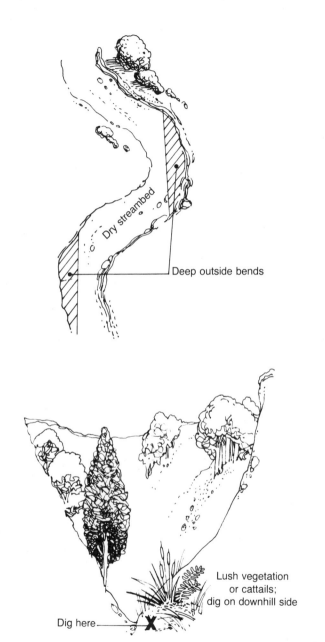

In a dry steambed you can often dig to find water in the deeper outside bends (top). In hilly terrain (bottom), look for springs where steep hillsides come together and there is lush vegetation.

First, consider the absence of readily visible water, as in the case of a dry stream bed or spring that no longer is producing. Often, water is still present, but due to lack of recent rainfall the underground water table has receded — so no surface accumulations. In this situation, find the point of lowest elevation in the immediate area and begin digging. After going down only 1 foot you'll probably encounter very damp soil, and somewhere between 2 and 3 feet deep water will slowly begin trickling in and filling the hole. It likely will be muddy water, but that's no problem (as we discuss in the next section).

If no dry wash or defunct spring can readily be found, search for the greenest, lushest vegetation you can find, then again find the point of lowest elevation nearby and begin digging.

In terrain that is particularly rocky, look for small depressions or dished-out holes where rainwater may have collected. Such places usually are leakproof and will hold water for surprisingly long periods. Since the only way it can escape is by evaporation, those collection basins located in shady places will hold water longest.

Building a solar collector also is a possibility, but you have to plan in advance and have necessary materials on hand. You must also be at an established camp and therefore have plenty of time to wait around, because even under optimum conditions the yield from such a device averages less than 2 quarts per day.

A solar collector is made by digging a hole that is 3 feet wide and 3 feet deep, then placing a collection pan in the bottom. The top of the hole is next covered with a sheet of clear plastic, held in place around the edges of the hole with rocks or sod. In the center of the plastic sheet place a baseball-size rock, which will cause the middle of the plastic to sag like a cone. The combination of the bright sun overhead and the damp earth beneath the plastic causes droplets of condensation to form on the bottom side of the sheet. The droplets of condensed moisture then run down the underslope of the plastic to the peak of the cone created by the rock; from there they drop, one by one, into the collection pan.

Retrieving the pan of water means disassembling the entire solar collector, so it is best to do this only once a day. Meanwhile, any time you want a drink, sip from a long, strawlike plastic tube that runs from the collection pan to the outside of the hole. Since this is a long distance to suck water, take one large inhaling breath, then pinch the tube, grab another breath, and continue sipping until you have your drink. The pinching effort keeps water drawn part way up the tube from draining back out while you take a breath.

A solar collector can produce more water if the hole you've dug is lined with any lush, green vegetation you can find in the immediate vicinity. To maintain the effectiveness of the solar collector, replace this vegetation every two days, or move the collector to a new place altogether since the water in the soil at each location will gradually become depleted.

In winter, water is everywhere, in the form of ice and snow. The only difficulty is the time-consuming effort of converting it from a solid to a liquid. With a conventional backpack trail stove, it can take forty-five minutes to melt down 1 gallon of snow to produce only 4 cups of drinkable water; if the water is to be used for cooking, it can take another ten to fifteen minutes to bring it to a boil. So if you have to melt any quantity of snow or ice, conserve your stove's fuel and build a fire.

Another tip when melting snow: Don't use too hot a flame on your stove's burner, or place your melting pot directly over robust flames, or you will scorch the snow. If there's no other alternative, add a bit of water to the bottom of the pot before putting in the snow.

In arid country, a solar collector will provide up to 2 quarts of pure water per day, but you must plan ahead and have on hand basic supplies for making the still.

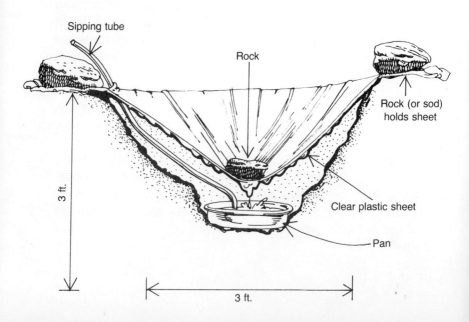

Sipping tube

Rock

Rock (or sod) holds sheet

3 ft.

Clear plastic sheet

Pan

3 ft.

Two other words of advice: First, if there is a snowbank several feet above an ice-free stream or river, don't risk climbing down to fill your water vessel. You may slip and go into the drink, and in freezing temperatures this can be traumatic (if not worse). It's better to tie a lightweight cord to your canteen or plastic bottle, throw it into the water, let it fill of its own accord, then hoist it out. Second, when drinking ice-cold water from a spring or stream during winter, do so slowly and only a small sip at a time. Otherwise, a painful bellyache may follow.

PURIFYING WATER

Finding adequate quantities of water seldom is so perplexing to a trail cook as making sure it is safe to drink or use in the preparation of meals. All kinds of germs and bacterial organisms too small to see may be present in the water, and if not reckoned with may ruin the entire outing by causing digestive upsets, nausea, or diarrhea. In extreme cases, the result may be dysentery, cholera, or typhoid.

Even crystal-clear water found in remote wilderness areas should be suspect. Never trust the tale about water purifying itself by rushing over rocks in sunlight, or about water you see wildlife drinking also being safe for human consumption. Neither of these bits of folklore has any basis of truth. Who knows what moose or bear passed through the region just moments before your arrival and perchance heeded the call of nature right where you are now filling your canteen?

The first order of business is to strain or filter the water to remove any visible debris that may be floating around. There are several ways of doing this, and one of the most ingenious is one I saw several years ago in northern Ontario. I was camped with some Cree Indians on the banks of the Oogitchi River where the walleye fishing was terrific. One night a cloudburst sent torrents of runoff water from steep hillsides into the river and in no time our drinking supply was muddied. Instead of collecting water from the river itself, guide Benny Simpson dug a hole in the sandy shoreline 3 feet from the water's edge. The hole quickly, amazingly, filled with clear water. The sandy bank had served as a makeshift filter. We simply ladled out what we needed.

A more practical way of removing sediment from water, if you have a large enought container, is to let it sit overnight to allow dirt particles and other suspended matter to settle gradually to the bottom. Many types of water vessels now on the market are perfectly suited to this. Some hold as much as 2 to 3 gallons and all are of very lightweight fabric or plastic, so they are easily collapsible for stowing in a pack.

One model is the Pocket Water Bag, from the L.L. Bean Company, Freeport, Maine 04033. It's made of urethane-coated ripstop nylon with a webbed carrying strap, holds over 3 gallons of water, yet weighs only 2 ounces and can be folded into a square about the size of a deck of cards. Vessels like this are also handy for hauling water from a stream or spring to the campsite, and even for bathing.

The fastest way to filter water is by using two containers, pouring the water from one through a piece of clean cotton cloth into the other. Even more effective is using one of those paper filters made for automatic drip-coffee makers; five of them weigh only an ounce and can be kept clean in a plastic sandwich bag.

Once the water is free of sediment and other debris, you have to kill any bacteria and germs and sterilize any microscopic matter that could prove harmful if ingested. A sure-fire way, literally, is to place a pot of water on a campstove or fire grate, bring it to a rolling boil and allow it to bubble

The best way to purify water is to boil it. To eliminate the flat taste this produces, aerate the water by vigorously stirring it, or pour it from one vessel to another.

away for a full ten minutes. It now is perfectly fine for drinking or cooking.

The ten-minute boiling time pertains only to purifying water at sea level, however. As altitude increases, the boiling point of water decreases, thereby requiring a longer time over the flame. A rule of thumb: Add one minute of boiling time for every 1,000-foot rise in elevation. In other words, boil the water thirteen minutes at 3,000 feet, fifteen minutes at 5,000, eighteen minutes at 8,000, and so on.

Another popular method of purification is adding Halazone tablets to the water. These are available through any pharmacy and come in 2-ounce bottles of 100. Usually, the recommended procedure is to add from two to four tablets (they are very tiny) to each quart of water, shake vigorously, and let stand for thirty minutes, but be sure to read carefully the instructions on the bottle first.

Halazone tablets work by releasing chlorine gas into the water, which kills bacterial organisms that may be harmful to good health. In semitropical and tropical climates, chlorine alone may be inadequate, in which case iodine water-purification tablets (also available in drugstores) should be substituted.

In either case, the potency of such tablets deteriorates with time; to ensure full strength, periodically check the expiration date listed on the bottle. If no such date is indicated, ask your pharmacist about the shelf life of the tablets, then calculate the expiration date yourself and write it on the bottle with indelible ink.

Both Halazone and iodine tablets should be stored in a waterproof container and out of direct sunlight. It generally is best just to leave them in their original dark-colored plastic bottles. Few times a backpacker is so restricted by weight limitations that he cannot slip the entire 2-ounce bottle into a side pocket of his knapsack where it always will be handy.

Moreover, you can also use conventional liquid iodine of the kind found in first aid kits, or liquid chlorine (in the form of the household bleach called Clorox). Add 5 drops of iodine to each quart of clear water (10 drops to cloudy water) and let stand for one-half hour. Or, add 10 drops of Clorox to each quart of clear water (15 drops to cloudy water) and let stand for one-half hour. Both chemicals are easily transported in a small, leakproof plastic bottle.

Halazone tablets are specially made for sportsmen. These two tab-lets will make a canteen of suspect water safe to drink within thirty minutes.

Whether you elect to use the boiling, Halazone, iodine, or chlorine treatments, the dissolved oxygen in the water will have become greatly depleted, giving it a flat, unpalatable taste. This is easily remedied by stirring the water vigorously a few minutes with a spoon to create lots of bub-bles. Or aerate the water by pouring it back and forth a dozen times from one container to another.

Recently, some of the major manufacturers of backpack-ing and camping gear have also gotten into the act by mak-ing available many types of portable water purification equipment. Eastern Mountain Sports produces a tablet called tetraglycine hydroperiodide; each tablet will purify 1 quart of water. This is very convenient: You need only pause at a stream, fill your canteen, add a "tetra-hydro" pill,

Many water purification gadgets on the market are well-suited to outdoor use. Here the author's wife, Marianne, uses the Super-Straw. Even polluted water is safe to drink when sucked through the tube, which contains a chemically treated charcoal filter.

continue hiking, and in thirty minutes you'll have safe drinkable water.

The same company also makes the Super Straw, which, along with the above chemical in liquid form, is especially handy when confronted with water that is both dirty and unsafe to drink. Fill your canteen or drinking cup with the water, add the required number of drops of tetra-hydro to kill all germs and bacteria, then insert the 6-inch-long plastic straw and sip. The straw contains a special filter to remove mud, dirt, sediment, agricultural pollutants, and even rust. Each Super Straw, which can ride handily in a shirt pocket, is capable of filtering up to 10 gallons of water before it needs to be replaced.

Still other water filtering and purification devices are somewhat larger than the Super Straw and intended for handling greater quantities of water for cooking. One is Portable Instapur made by Water Pic. Look for it in drugstores or in the Laacke & Joys Camping Catalog, 1432 North Water Street, Milwaukee, Wisconsin 53202. Portable Instapur is about the same size as a thermos and contains a chemically treated charcoal element. You pour contaminated water in top and it drains out the bottom ready to drink or use in cooking. The unit will purify 50 gallons of water before a replacement filter must be installed.

A similar gizmo, also shaped like a thermos, is the Water Treatment Unit made by Palco Products, 3017 San Fernando Road, Los Angeles, California 90065. I really like this one because it collapses to the size of a drinking cup and weighs only 1 pound. What's more, it will treat up to 1,000 gallons.

To purify large quantities of water, consider a unit such as Palco's Water Treatment Bottle. It weighs 1 pound, collapses to convenient carrying size, and will purify up to 1,000 gallons before the filter inside must be replaced.

Then there is the almost identical Water Washer Treatment Unit made by American Water Purification, Inc., 115 Mason Circle, Concord, California 94520. This model is also shaped like a thermos, weighs 16 ounces, has an internal filtering system used in conjunction with a chemical tablet, and will purify 1,000 gallons of water before the filter must be replaced.

8

Cooking Over Fire

Almost since man's beginning, fire has played a major role in his comfort. Flickering tongues of flame warm the body, and the soul, by keeping the darkness and creeping shadows at bay. And food prepared over glowing embers to the melody of birdsong simply cannot be compared to that which merely is heated on the burner of a gas or electric range at home. Yet, as more people take to the outdoors every year, the landscape can ill afford to have everyone hacking away at live trees, indiscriminately building fires wherever they please, and then leaving charred reminders of their visit to greet the next party that passes through.

The true mark of an accomplished outdoorsman and expert trail cook therefore is the ability to gather materials without wreaking havoc upon the terrain, cook a meal over a fire that is entirely safe, enjoy the crimson flames into the late-night hours, then press on the following morning leaving no indication that his camp had ever been there.

My friend Nick Duggan is one such trail chef, and I defy anyone to follow a day or two behind him and accurately determine his random cooking sites. You may discover a temporarily matted place in the buffalo grass where Nick lay in his sleeping bag, but never his "kitchen."

When Duggan recently guided me on an elk hunt in Wyoming's Grand Tetons, I naturally paid special attention to his cooking skills. One tool he often used was a common shovel. Not only was it handy around the cooking fire but it also came into play for digging our latrine, a hole for disposing dishwater, and still another for roasting meat underground in a cast-iron dutch oven.

If this sounds like excessively heavy equipment to be taking into the wilderness for trail cooking, I'll confess we were leading two packhorses as we hiked. We needed the animals to lug 400 pounds of boned elk meat out of the backcountry, so we took advantage of the circumstances by outfitting ourselves with additional cooking gear, too. In other situations, just the ticket might be a lightweight Army-surplus entrenching tool, a small shovel that folds in half for easy storage and weighs only 2½ pounds.

Nick Duggan's fire-building expertise is worth describing because many of his preferred techniques are readily adaptable to any type of trail cooking.

In Nick's mind, the initial task in setting camp is selecting the proper cooking site. In fact, once water is located, Duggan scouts the immediate area for just that, and not for the perfect place to pitch his tent, as do most campers.

This strategy served Nick well in setting up his camp kitchen: Build a fire away from overhanging tree branches or large swatches of brush or other dry cover. They could be ignited by a stray spark swept away by the wind.

Carefully evaluate the ground itself. Spend the time to find hard-packed mineral soil, then remove the top couple of inches with a shovel and set it aside. (When you don't have a shovel or entrenching tool, use the inverted edge-like rim of your frying pan as you would a hoe.) This surface removal of debris is important. In many forested and grassland regions, generations of tree-leaf litter and other dead vegetation have made a thick carpet of peat or "duff" that won't burn readily but will harbor the smallest spark, allowing it just barely to smolder for days or even weeks. Many an inexperienced camper has thought his campfire was entirely extinguished, left the area, and an unnoticed spark traveling underground among roots and dead pine needles has eventually popped up, perhaps dozens of yards away, and ignited dry grass or leaves.

Clear a 4- or 5-foot circle to bare soil, then build a fire ring with rocks, or a rectangular affair from green logs, the rocks or logs to contain flames, coals, and ashes. Be sure to use only dry rocks such as smooth, hard granite. Soft, porous rocks such as sandstone, or those gathered from a damp lowland or old stream bed, may contain moisture. When the rocks become hot, the internal build-up of steam pressure may eventually make them explode.

To break camp, follow these procedures:

- Drench the entire cooking area thoroughly with water.
- Carry the rocks away from the immediate site and randomly scatter them with their blackened sides down. The scorched marks are nothing more than carbon stains that are quickly absorbed by the soil and growing vegetation. Conversely, blackened portions of rocks left face up are an eyesore, and it may take years of wind and rain to weather them slowly back to their natural appearances.
- Remove any larger log from the fire area and place it, too, charred side down.
- Leave the remaining ashes and any cold remnants of unburned wood in the fire pit, and shovel the thin surface layer of sod previously scraped away carefully back in place. Tamp it down, and sprinkle with a covering of duff.

Veteran trail cooks don't select campsites based on convenient places to pitch their tents. They first look for water, then the ideal cooking site. Note how ground has been cleared of leaves and other debris with a lightweight shovel, and the actual cooking area enclosed by rocks.

All of this takes a few minutes of extra effort, but, as I said, another group of hunters or campers may arrive days later and never suspect someone has been there shortly before them.

A couple of exceptions override the usual rules of fire-site selection. If someone has thoughtlessly left a fire ring of blackened rocks near a spot you deem slightly better, use the same site your predecessor did. That's better than constructing an entirely different cooking area only yards away. Then, before leaving, try to restore the area to its natural appearance so those who follow you can enjoy it fully.

Another situation occurs on lands administered by agencies such as the U.S. Forest Service or state departments of natural resources, in which specific cooking or fire-building sites have been designated and campers are strongly discouraged, or even prohibited, from building fires elsewhere. Often, cooking grates made from steel rods have been imbedded into the earth or into concrete frameworks intended, I suppose, to resemble barbecues. Or you may find some type of fire ring made from a circular piece of 12-inch-high welded sheet metal, with a grate on top made from steel rods. By the looks and dimensions of most of these grillwork assemblies and other contraptions, I am convinced the people who designed and built them are the most inept outdoor cooks in the world. About the only course of action is to shake your head in disbelief, shrug your shoulders, humor them, and choke down the resulting meal.

BUILDING THE FIRE

Many tenderfeet labor under the misconception that a large fire belching roaring flames is necessary for trail cooking. Nothing could be farther from the truth.

Actually, there are two types of fires used in most camps, each serving distinctly different purposes and thereby fed with unlike fuels. One is the social fire you sit around at night and poke with a stick while swapping fishing tales and other yarns. This type of fire also bathes the campsite in a soft, illuminating glow and sometimes provides a modicum of heat. Here, robust flames are indeed desired. They are best obtained with coniferous softwoods that contain a lot of resinous tars, or hardwoods of low molecular density that burn relatively hot and fast, such as willow, birch, and aspen.

Fires for cooking are a world apart. High flames are not desired (except for reflector-oven cooking, discussed in Chapter 12). Nor do you want to use any of the pine, spruce, or fir species for the actual cooking (for starting fires, yes) because the pitch and resin in the wood leave the food tasting like turpentine. What you do want is an easily manageable bed of coals, similar to the charcoal cooking done in your backyard at home. Obviously, charcoal is much too heavy to carry in a pack, so firewood must be gathered on location and then transformed into suitable cooking coals.

Excellent woods for cooking, although they are not easy to start, are dense hardwoods such as hickory, oak, maple, and locust, or the slightly less dense, pleasingly aromatic fruitwoods such as apple or cherry. (Whatever the wood, strip off the bark, if possible; when burning, it sometimes releases a musky odor that can make your food smell like a moldy old mattress.)

The first step in fire building begins with tinder. Every successful fire requires fuel, oxygen, and kindling temperature. Kindling temperature is achieved through the use of tinder, which ignites easily and in turn raises the kindling temperature of twigs and then succeeding layers of progressively larger sizes of branches and other pieces of wood.

CHARACTERISTICS OF VARIOUS WOODS

Species	Ease of Starting	Cooking Qualities	Sparks	Smoke	Imparted Flavors
Apple	Difficult	Excellent	Few	Little	Excellent
Ash	Fair	Good	Few	Little	Good
Aspen	Fair	Fair	Moderate	Little	Good
Beech	Difficult	Good	Few	Little	Good
Birch	Easy	Fair	Moderate	Moderate	Good
Cedar	Easy	Poor	Many	Heavy	Bad
Cherry	Difficult	Excellent	Few	Little	Excellent
Elm	Fair	Poor	Few	Heavy	Bad
Fir	Easy	Poor	Many	Heavy	Bad
Hickory	Difficult	Excellent	Moderate	Little	Excellent
Locust	Difficult	Excellent	Few	Little	Good
Maple	Difficult	Excellent	Few	Little	Excellent
Oak	Difficult	Excellent	Few	Little	Good
Pine	Easy	Poor	Many	Heavy	Bad
Spruce	Easy	Poor	Many	Heavy	Bad
Sycamore	Difficult	Poor	Moderate	Moderate	Bad

Tinder consists of almost anything that is readily combustible — toothpick-size twigs, shavings whittled from dry sticks, dry leaves, dead grass, scraps of birch bark, a crumpled piece of paper, dead pine needles, even an old bird's nest. Gather a good quantity of any of these materials and fluff them up in a small pile in the center of your fire ring.

Next, loosely stack on top in crisscross or tepee fashion a number of sticks of pencil-diameter size, followed by more the diameter of your thumb, and then still more of broom-handle size, insuring all the while they are not too tightly packed together, to allow the free flow of oxygen. These woods may consist of fast-burning hardwoods such as willow or softwoods such as pine or spruce; as I noted earlier, none of them is well suited to cooking, but in the

The key to successful fire building is to begin with tinder and then use graduated sizes of dry hardwoods. Anything with a diameter larger than your wrist takes too long to reduce to coals.

When natural tinder is scarce, you can create your own with a fuzz-stick. Use dry softwood and whittle shavings, but do not cut them entirely free of the main stem. Then stack several fuzz-sticks in teepee or log-cabin fashion to produce a quick blaze.

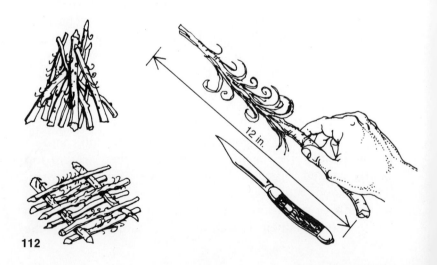

12 in.

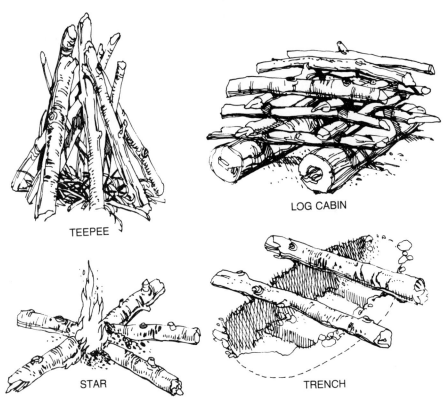

TEEPEE

LOG CABIN

STAR

TRENCH

Fire designs are numerous. For starting fires, the teepee and log-cabin designs are the most popular. For a social fire at night, use the star design to conserve fuel by pushing the spokes into the central fire zone. For cooking, especially in windy weather, dig a trench for the fire and then lay green logs on top to support pots and pans.

beginning what's important is to establish a quick, hot-burning fire that will raise the kindling temperature of the less easily combustible hardwoods to be added later.

As soon as you have a hot fire, begin adding pieces of oak, hickory, cherry, or others, first of 1-inch diameter and then approximately wrist-size diameter. (If the diameter is larger, it will take an eternity for the logs to reduce themselves to white-ash coals for cooking.)

Once the hardwoods are going strong, Nick Duggan and other veteran trail cooks like to begin to attend to various chores around camp, such as collecting and purifying water, pitching the tent, unrolling sleeping bags, and so on. This allows ample time for the fire to burn itself gradually down to the point at which the undesirable woods used to start the fire are entirely consumed, and the hardwoods nothing but glowing embers for cooking. After the meal is finished, you lay several pieces of softwoods or less densely grained hardwoods on the coals to quickly reestablish your flames for the evening social fire.

Type of fires. Often the design of the fire is determined by the type of cooking to be done or accessory equipment you plan to use. For example, when I'm traveling extremely light, with no room in my pack for grill to set pots and pans upon, I like to build my fire in a stacked, crisscross, log-cabin lay. Once a bed of coals has been generated, I take two green logs, each about 3 inches in diameter by 2 feet long, place them on opposite sides of the coals, then push them toward each other so they are only about 6 inches apart. This has the effect of nudging the coals into a rectangular bed, and the logs are usually close together to support a frying pan or kettle.

If you have some type of lightweight grill along, use the same approach but leave the two green logs 8 to 12 inches apart. The same applies when using a grill set on rocks encircling the fire. When using rocks without grill, you can usually arrange a couple of rocks here and there to support a pot or skillet.

From past (angering) experiences, I no longer place much confidence in the countless methods of using "dingle" sticks held in place by rocks to suspend cook pots over the fire. Nor do I favor the idea of two forked sticks driven into the ground, which are supposed to support a third cross-member from which pots hang from "hooks" whittled from

A simple variation of the trench fire is to make a log-cabin or teepee fire, and when the wood has burned down to coals, use two green logs to straddle the embers. Put pots and pans on top.

still other sticks. In Boy Scout handbooks, drawings of these gimmicks are enchanting, born of masters of the art of woodcraft. In practice, they pose many drawbacks. Too much time is wasted searching for the right-size sticks and branches and then fashioning them to proper dimensions with a hatchet or knife. Once they are in place, it's an exercise in frustration trying to readjust their heights in relation to the coals. This is sometimes necessary to regulate the desirable amount of heat under the food. These contrap-

A tripod arrangement allows you to regulate the heat for cooking.
Here, hunters broil venison steaks in Colorado's White River
National Forest.

tions also have the unnerving habit of falling over, breaking,
or burning through from the heat of the fire and dumping
one's dinner into the ashes.

However, there are a few exceptions — one, a neat idea
frequently used by my friend Mike Wolter of St. Paul, Minnesota. Mike's philosophy is "why fight the fire" by periodically trying to control its fluctuating temperatures? Why not
just raise or lower the grillwork accordingly, by means of a
small S-hook in the links of an overhead chain? It works
like a charm.

He builds his fire inside a ring of rocks and then contrives
an overhead tripod from three stout, green sticks about 3
inches in diameter. They stand about 6 feet high and are
fastened at the apex with several wraps of wire. From the

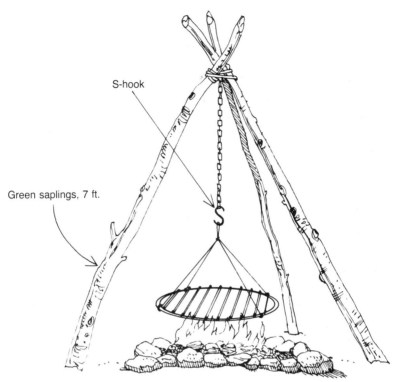

S-hook

Green saplings, 7 ft.

To make your own tripod grill, use green saplings 8 feet long and secured at the apex with strong wire. A lightweight length of chain hanging from the peak supports the light grillwork, but the important element is the small S-hook for adjusting height.

peak of the tripod hangs a very lightweight chain or stout wire. Midway along its length three other segments of wire or chain are joined and in turn attached to the grill.

Although this idea is not suited to very lightweight trail tramping or "quickie" overnight camps, it's a cunning arrangement when your stay in a given area is of several days duration. Moreover, it's ideal when there are several members in the party; larger required quantities of food can be prepared this way, and there are a couple of additional strong backs to carry the weight.

The most versatile fire design is the venerable "keyhole lay," named after its shape. With a robust fire in the circular portion, you can regulate heat by raking coals as needed into the rectangular cooking area.

The Mirro Cookware Company, P.O. Box 409, Manitowoc, Wisconsin 54220 offers a factory-made version of Mike Wolter's hanging-tripod grill idea on behalf of those who would rather buy one instead of fabricating their own. The complete Mirro outfit, including the tripod, grill and adjustable chainwork, weighs 9 pounds and disassembles for easy carrying.

This matter of careful temperature regulation for cooking various foods over fire is important in another way, as well. Some freeze-dried or dehydrated backpack foods reconstituted with water have to be brought to a boil and then simmered for a specified length of time, so the temperature must be significantly reduced. Some other dry foods are supposed to be boiled for the entire duration of their cooking time. Then there are a wide number of foods that are precooked and need only be warmed before serving. Naturally, since there are no temperature dials on an open fire, either the distance between the food and the fire, or the intensity of the fire itself, are the only means of regulating the heat. Occasionally adjusting the height of the grill is the easiest way of changing the distance between the food and the coals.

There are two ways of adjusting the intensity of the fire itself. One is no more complicated than now and then flicking water droplets on the coals. This also is the recommended procedure for squelching any flames that may spew up if food drippings fall upon the coals. A more sophisticated method of temperature regulation goes back to our mention of various cooking-fire designs. I'm thinking mainly of one brainstorm some astute trail cook invented long ago called the "keyhole lay," undoubtedly the most versatile approach to trail cooking ever conceived.

Prepare the cook site by using rocks to create the outline of an old-fashioned keyhole as viewed from directly above: There should be a circular fire pit about 2 feet in diameter that is entirely ringed with rocks, with a narrow, rock-outlined rectangular arm at one side. In the circular area, build a robust fire from wood such as dry willow and keep a good quantity of replacement kindling nearby. Then, with a type of rake fashioned from a forked stick, or your shovel, pull needed quantities of glowing coals from the fire into the rectangular area for cooking. If and when the cooking coals begin to cool, replenish them with more dragged out of the main fire. If the heat becomes too high, or should be lowered because of the type of food you're preparing, push some of the coals out of the rectangular area back into the main fire where they will keep until you need them again.

COOKING GRILLS AND ACCESSORIES

As already mentioned, trail cooking over an open fire carries with it a good deal of personal responsibility and an environmentally conscientious attitude to match. In addition to preparing a fire site that is completely safe, and then restoring the appearance of the terrain before leaving, every effort should be made to ensure that living trees are not damaged.

There are few justifiable reasons for cutting green wood. One instance might be to fashion a tripod to support a hanging grill, or to provide two pieces of wood close enough to glowing coals to support pots and pans without burning through. But in these and similar situations it usually is possible to find a tree knocked down by high winds or one that is obviously dying but still possesses a few green branches. For all other fire-building and cooking duties, the most easily accessible wood, the best for cooking, and that which is ecologically the most acceptable choice is that which is dead, thoroughly dry, and just lying about.

For reducing larger pieces of wood in this category to suitable cooking size, some trail cooks like to bring along a lightweight belt hatchet. If the extra weight is no problem, that's fine; but most times I simply subscribe to the belief that if the wood is too large to be broken by hand, or by stomping upon it with my boots, it's too large for efficient trail cooking. You should easily be able to break dry, dead wood of wrist-size diameter. Forget about the rest, unless nothing else is available.

You're certain to encounter a time or two when all the wood on the ground is wet from a previous rain or a combination of sleet and snow. Look around and you'll probably find dead wood that is still standing and is sure to be much drier. Then, as added insurance, use larger quantities of tinder than usual, as well as the pencil-size and thumb-size

The author's favorite fire starter is Mautz Fire Ribbon. Squeeze the jellied alcohol onto wood like toothpaste and then light with a match. Incredibly, the Fire Ribbon will burn even on water, ice, or snow and ignite the wettest wood.

woods to follow. Even after the most torrential downpour, pine needles, brittle twigs, and bark from trees standing in thick groves should be relatively dry (even more so the twigs and needles closest to the ground). So will the insides of larger pieces of dead wood, although you'll need a hatchet to split them open. In a wilderness survival class I took at Fort Benning, Georgia, I once saw a floating log retrieved from a lake, split open, and the heartwood used to start a fire. This confirms the tenet that burnable wood is around for anyone who's imaginative enough to find it.

Another bit of insurance can be purchased in your local camping-supply store in the form of endless gadgets for fire starting. From my experience, the most reliable consist of tubes containing a flammable, jellied alcohol that can be squeezed onto wet wood like toothpaste and will burn long enough to dry the sticks and bring them to kindling temper-

Palco's Metal Match works in damp weather when fires are difficult to ignite.

ature. The one I like best is called Mautz Fire Ribbon. It produces no dangerous flare-up, is odorless, will not affect foods later cooked over the fire, and actually burns on water, snow, or ice.

Then there is the venerable Metal Match made by Palco Products; it consists of a small rod that can be struck against any metal surface (such as your knife blade) and subsequently will ignite just like a wooden kitchen match. Each Metal Match is capable of starting up to 1,000 fires.

I also like Coghlan's Magnesium Fire Starter. This consists of a small, rectangular, magnesium bar. To use it, first shave off a small pile of dust particles with your knife blade. Then turn the bar over and briskly strike your knife blade against a special rod located on the opposite side; this causes sparks to fly off and quickly ignite the pile of magnesium shavings.

All three of these products (Mautz Fire Ribbon, Metal Match, and Magnesium Fire Starter), as well as similar

Coghlan's Magnesium Strike Rod weighs only 1 ounce, and is capable of starting hundreds of fires when tinder is unavailable. **Step 1:** Gather pencil-size twigs.

Step 2: Use the blade of your knife to scrape shavings from edge of magnesium rod.

Step 3: Turn the rod over and use your knife blade to "whittle" sparks briskly from the attached sparking insert. The shavings will instantly ignite into a very hot flame that will start larger pieces of wood.

others, are listed in most mail-order camping-supply catalogs and can also be found in backpacking shops.

I've already suggested that a compact shovel of sorts comes in handy around any cooking fire. But if you'd prefer not to have the flopping weight of an axe on your belt, why

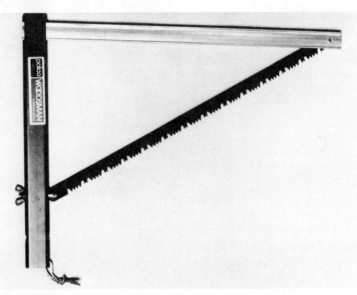

Reducing wood to size can be accomplished with a belt axe, but much more convenient is a lightweight Swedish saw that folds into its handle. Cut only dead, dry wood for cooking.

A lightweight shovel is invaluable around the cooking site. The collapsible entrenching tool weighs only 1½ pounds.

Lightweight wire grills abound. Choose one depending on how much weight you can carry and the sizes of your cooking implements. You can even make your own grill, like the one shown at the left.

not look into the many types of lightweight, folding Swedish saws now on the market?

Another invaluable item is a small section of lightweight wire grill. You may be able to salvage a shelf from a discarded oven or refrigerator at the local junkyard and with a hacksaw cut it to convenient carrying size ($12'' \times 14''$ is just right). Since many of these shelves are treated with a zinc or cadmium cladding, good advice is to burn the grill at home for an hour over a very hot bed of charcoal to remove the surface coating that otherwise may impart your food with a bad taste.

There also are several variations of wire backpacking grills on the market that weigh scant ounces. With some, stiff wire legs can be unfolded and then pressed into the earth to hold the grill elevated over your coals. Another type is simply a rectangular grill made of tubular aluminum measuring 5″ × 14″ that can be laid across rocks or logs to support two pots or pans. This little beauty, a distinct favorite with go-light advocates, weighs only 4 ounces.

9

Trail Stoves

From an outdoorsman's perspective, few things in life can match the happiness of waking at dawn to the mixed aromas of blue woodsmoke, perking coffee, and bacon crackling in a frying pan. You unzip your sleeping bag, poke your head through the tent flaps, and there is your partner huddled over coals dancing with tiny flames as he alternately cracks eggs into a skillet and warms his hands against the morning chill. Immediately you know that no matter what may be happening thousands of miles away, at least here in this place all is right with the world. Most sportsmen wouldn't hear of establishing a camp in the backcountry without a campfire being an integral part of the setting.

But, aside from the joy and satisfaction of cooking over fire, sometimes it's impossible or at best impractical:

- You're photographing mountain goats far above timberline, for example, and not a stick of wood is within miles.

- You're right at timberline, following a timeworn game trail to a little-known lake where golden trout have grown fat and sassy. Unfortunately, for as far as the eye can see,

Many times cooking over a campfire is not convenient. The modern backpacking stove fills the void when it's raining, when firewood is unavailable, or when you merely want to heat a few ounces of water to make a soup or stew.

the "timber" is ponderosa pine, which rates one notch higher than petrified sheep dung when it comes to preferred cooking fuels.

- You're hiking the Appalachian Trail through portions of several eastern states. But the season has been terribly dry, the hills and woodlands are like a tinderbox, and in most regions the Forest Service or state departments of natural resources have enacted temporary bans on open fires.

- You're on a combination camping and rock-hounding mission along the northern shore of Lake Superior in early spring. Everything is sopping wet from four solid days of rain. If you were in a survival situation you could manage a fire, but just for cooking it would prove to be a royal pain in the *gluteus maximus*.

- Weather conditions are perfect, and everywhere you look there is plenty of dry wood. But you're en route from one place to another and stopping only briefly for lunch. All you need to heat is eight ounces of water to reconstitute a package of freeze-dried beef and noodles. You don't want to go through the entire ritual of gathering wood, preparing a fire site, and all the rest, just to bring two cups of water to a boil.

There are other situations, as well, when an outdoorsman has to forego building a fire.

Enter the popular backpack stoves, most of which are inexpensive, incredibly lightweight, easy to operate, and can be put into service at a moment's notice. Some types work as efficiently as your gas range at home; you merely turn a dial and strike a match. With them, you can prepare an elegant shrimp-creole dinner in the evening, or a cup of

Modern trail stoves are lightweight, durable, of exceptionally high quality, and easy to use. This model by Coleman comes housed in its own case, which doubles as a 1-quart pot.

tea at noon. Use them on a sun-drenched hillside in mid-summer, on a rocky, snow-covered crag in winter, or inside your tent when thunderclaps and Mother Nature turns the faucet wide open. In fact, modern backpacking stoves are so versatile it would be a ponderous chore to list times when they cannot be used. And that explains why the vast majority of trail trampers always have one type or another in their duffle, not necessarily to be used as the sole means of meal preparation but to complement cooking over coals when conditions occasionally are not favorable to fire building.

STOVE FUELS

Dozens of lightweight stoves on the market are perfect for trail use. Since virtually every one I have ever tested has been of very high-quality construction, it seems the question of which fuel to use probably is more important than the specific brand name or stove design itself.

The five most common fuels are white gasoline, kerosene, butane, propane, and alcohol. Weigh the advantages and disadvantages of each, then decide which is most compatible with your own pilgrimages in the outdoors. You may even find yourself purchasing two stoves, each using a different type of fuel, to be put into use as the seasons change, or the menu or number of people in the party.

White gasoline. There is no question that white gas (or the similar Coleman fuel, which can be used as a substitute) is the most popular across North America. The advantages of white gas: it is widely available, even in remote regions; when burned it produces a very hot flame; accidently spilled fuel quickly evaporates; it is comparatively inexpensive; it's one of the best possible fuels for cold-weather cooking; and the same fuel for the stove is used as the necessary priming agent. The drawbacks of white gas are that priming is required, by burning a couple of teaspoons of the fuel in a preheating cup, which serves to warm the tank and vaporize the gasoline. Also, accidently spilled fuel is very flammable, the bottom of the tank of a self-pressurizing stove must be insulated from snow or cold ground for the unit to operate efficiently (use a slab of bark or a small square of ensolite), and such stoves are sometimes difficult to light or use in high winds.

Kerosene. In addition to being readily available across North America, kerosene can easily be found in Europe, the Scandinavian countries, South America, and most other parts of the world. Other advantages: spilled fuel will not readily ignite; Btu heat output is high; a kerosene stove can be set directly on snow or cold ground and still operate efficiently; stoves that have pump-pressure systems have reduced priming times; and the fuel is inexpensive compared to some others. On the negative side, kerosene stoves tend to be a bit heavier than some others, spilled fuel does not quickly evaporate, priming is required, and there may be difficulty operating them in strong winds.

Butane. Butane stoves use fuel canisters about the same size and shape as aerosol cans of shaving cream. The main plus here is that once a fuel canister is screwed into place, all that's necessary to begin cooking is to turn the on/off valve and strike a match to the burner. This means no priming is required to achieve immediate heat output, although the Btus afforded by butane are substantially less than from white gas or kerosene. Butane stoves also are remarkably safe because there is no liquid fuel to spill. With butane, however, many believe the disadvantages far outnumber the positive features. For one, butane fuel cartridges are not widely available; the most common source is backpacking and camping stores, which are in short supply beyond the city-limits signs. Butane also is very expensive. The fuel cans themselves are somewhat heavy and present a disposal problem along the trail. On an extended outing, you'll be lugging around empty (but still heavy) fuel cans until you return to the trailhead or home where you can get rid of them. Another major problem with butane is that it becomes increasingly less efficient in terms of heat output as the temperature drops, and when the mercury falls below 32°F the fuel will not vaporize or ignite at all (the exception is one unique butane stove we'll examine later). Finally, with some brands of butane stoves the fuel canister cannot be removed until it is completely empty, which makes the stove-canister combination awkward for stowing in your pack.

Propane. Sometimes known in North America as LP gas, and throughout Europe as "Camping Gaz," propane is second in popularity only to white gas. It is almost identical to butane regarding advantages and disadvantages, but there are several notable differences. Many types of propane canisters can be refilled when empty. This, along with its more widespread availability (you can find it even in hardware and general-merchandise stores), means it is not quite as expensive as butane (though still significantly more costly than white gas or kerosene). An advantage that propane and butane stoves share is that if you run out of fuel while cooking, all you have to do is quickly unscrew the exhausted canister and slip in a fresh one. With white gas, safety considerations require the stove be allowed to cool down entirely before any refueling attempt is made; during the interim, some freeze-dried or dehydrated foods can become soggy.

Propane and butane fuels come in pressurized bottles about the size of shaving-cream cans. They are incredibly easy to use— simply turn a dial and touch a match to the burner head—but are inefficient in very cold weather.

Alcohol. Alcohol stoves are occasionally found in use in the outback, but they are by far the least popular. On the positive side, spilled alcohol evaporates quickly, any fire that perchance occurs can be put out with water, no priming is required to achieve instant heat, the stove assemblies themselves are typically very lightweight, and flames generated are quite stable and uniform under windy conditions. On the negative side, alcohol is expensive, and highly volatile if spilled, and when burned the resulting heat-output is discouragingly low. Also, most alcohol stoves presently on the market offer very limited control of heat settings.

Considering the five most commonly used fuels, I vote for propane stoves during mild to warm weather, when outings are of only two or three days' duration at most. These stoves are the picture of simplicity, you can get by with only one fuel cartridge, and nothing is better suited to beginners or sportsmen who want to attend to cooking quickly and then be on their way. For all other trail cooking, especially during colder weather and for outings lasting more than two or three days, I use white gas exclusively.

Before I look at specific stove brands, a few other words of advice on fuels:

• If you're using propane or butane and find yourself confronted with a sudden cold snap, keep your fuel canister and/or stove wrapped in your sleeping bag to keep it relatively warm and thereby improve the stove's efficiency. Also, if possible, cook inside your tent where the temperature is sure to be at least a few degrees warmer.

• Storing and transporting liquid fuels, such as white gas, kerosene, and alcohol, should receive careful thought. I like Sigg or Markhill fuel bottles. These are cylindrical, and available in ½-pint, pint, and quart sizes. They are made of very lightweight spun aluminum and have positive sealing, no-leak screw caps with gaskets. In conjunction with them, it's wise to bring along a small aluminum or plastic funnel for filling stove founts without spillage. You can also buy a pour cap to fit the bottle at a camping-supply store. Another good alternative is fuel flasks that are available through camping-supply dealers. These are flat, rectangular, and made of tinned steel. They are very easy to pack and have small, built-in pouring spouts, which eliminate the need for a funnel.

- Priming stoves, in order to vaporize liquid fuels, can be messy to use, also dangerous if excessive fluid is spilled on stove components. The safe way is to use a small eyedropper made for priming and available through outlets that sell trail stoves.

- Exercise precautions when cooking inside a tent. In addition to the obvious danger of igniting bedrolls, clothing, or other gear, provisions must be made for adequate ventilation to prevent the accumulation of toxic carbon-monoxide fumes.

To store and transport liquid fuels, use only durable, no-leak metal bottles. The one on the left is made of German tinned steel, the one on the right of spun aluminum. Lightweight plastic funnel prevents spillage; a wire screen inside the funnel filters the fuel of any sediment.

COMPARING TRAIL STOVES

There is a lightweight stove to suit everyone's needs. Yet everyone must make his or her own choice because the stove that is just right for you may be an abomination for me, and probably vice versa. As we have just seen, one crucial matter is the type of fuel the stove will operate on. This decided, the field is somewhat narrowed, but still other "weighty" factors have to be considered; at one extreme, the flyweight 3½-*ounce* Trangia alcohol stove, and at the other the hefty 3½-*pound* Optimus 111B gasoline model. In between are dozens more of intermediate sizes and weights.

The main thing to ponder here, after fuel type, is the average length of your journeys throughout the year, the complexity of your menus, and the number of pals that generally come along with you. If most of your outings are just you and your clodhoppers, and you're going as light as possible and preparing relatively simple meals, the Svea 123R white-gas stove may fill the bill in spades. This is a compact little job that is extremely durable and performs like a workhorse under the most demanding conditions. Only 4½ inches in diameter by 5 inches tall, with a small pot that doubles as a carrying case, the Svea holds 4 ounces of fuel and will bring an 8-ounce pan of water to a boil in approximately six minutes.

Let's say, however, that a buddy will be joining you on most of the outings and consequently your cooking vessels will have to be a bit larger to accommodate double-serving portions. Now, Coleman's Peak 1 white-gas stove is ideal. Relatively new on the market, the Peak 1 has already received international acclaim. Fold-out tripod legs make it much more stable than many other stand-up stoves. An X-shaped windscreen made from lightweight sheet-metal struts that crisscross the burner head make the stove easy to light and the heat easy to regulate, even in half-gale

Dozens of lightweight trail stoves on the market offer a variety of special features. Many are housed in their own containers that double as pots and pans. This model, the Optimus 99, runs on white gas and comes with a special windscreen.

A beauty for use in inclement weather, the Optimus 88N Storm-Proof, is a combination stove and cooking kit. On only ¼ pint of fuel, this model burns continually for 1¾ hours.

Test a trail stove in your back-yard, not after dark in the backcountry. This is the Purist 1, a recent addition to the Optimus line.

Kerosene stoves generally are heavier than those using other fuels, but their saving grace is their efficiency in below-freezing temperatures.

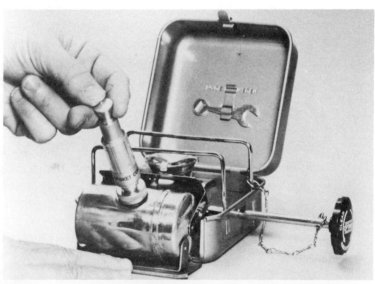

Many types of trail stoves can be fitted with special pressure pumps that increase their efficiency in cold weather when liquid fuels do not vaporize as quickly.

weather conditions. Also, the burner control is so well engineered that adjusting the heat from mild simmer to full boil, or anything in between, is easily done with one's fingertips.

Other impressive stand-up stoves include the venerable Optimus 45 kerosene model, Hank Robert's Propane Mini-Stove, and the Phoenix Mountaineer, which runs on white gas.

Then there is a wide variety of what I call "flat stoves" with low, fold-out silhouettes that are extremely stable. For multi-purpose cooking, I've already mentioned the large Optimus 111B, which measures 7 inches square by 4 inches high. This is a universal favorite among trail trampers since it is easily capable of cooking for three or four. For those who scowl at the Optimus 111B's 3½-pound weight, there is a junior version called the Optimus 8R that looks almost identical but tips the scale at a scant 1 pound, 9 ounces.

Numerous domestic and foreign companies now manufacture trail stoves, with each firm producing as many as five or six different models. So it pays to spend some time in your local outfitter's shop looking at what's available, or thumbing through the catalogs of camping mail-order houses that stock competitive brands.

The chart included here will enable you to compare features of some of the most popular models and decide which stove (or stoves) is best tailored to your outdoor-cooking needs.

Along with inspecting a stove's dimensions, fuel capacity, operating time, and other features, spend some time evaluating the individual designs of stoves themselves. When small burner heads are put into service, for example, even mild winds can make lighting difficult and greatly increase the required length of cooking time. To solve this, many types of stoves have built-in windscreens to block annoying breezes. Others are made in such a way that the top

In windy weather your trail stove will be more efficient if you shelter it within a horeshoe-shaped ring of rocks to block out annoying breezes.

lid of the stove's carrying case tips back on hinges to serve as a windscreen, and still others offer windscreens as optional equipment for those who more often than not find themselves cooking in wide open spaces where wind is more prevalent. Another alternative is merely to shelter your stove when cooking by placing it in the middle of a horseshoe-shaped ring of rocks, behind a toppled tree trunk, or behind two packframes propped upright.

I tend to like stoves that are housed in some types of lightweight aluminum case that also can serve as a cook pan. Otherwise, it's necessary to bring more cooking gear, and when on the trail somehow ensure the stove is protected from damage—and that gear and plastic bags are at the same time protected from the stove's various protrusions.

Two unique stoves deserve special mention. One is the Optimus 731 "Mouse Trap Stove" fueled with a small propane canister. I said earlier that propane and butane for the most part are not efficient in cold weather, due to their inability to vaporize properly when the temperature dips below 32°F. Well, the Optimus 731 is a nonconformist. Because of a special wick inside its companion fuel canister and an ingenious tube that preheats the gas before it reaches the burner, this is one propane stove that will operate down to 15°F, ordinarily propane's freezing point.

Another major breakthrough in trail-stove technology is the Mountain Safety Research MSR Multi-Fuel Stove. The beauty of this little gem is that it will operate efficiently on white gasoline, unleaded automotive gasoline, Coleman fuel, kerosene, No. 1 diesel fuel, and No. 1 coal oil. Infinitely versatile, it may be just what you're looking for if your outdoor tracks wind through random states (or foreign countries) where fuel availability and types are limited or diverse.

Operating tips. This potpourri of advice pertains to the use, maintenance, and cleaning of various trail stoves, as well as ways to improve their performance, and safety tips.

• Pretest a new stove before hitting the trail with it. Late at night, when it's dark and raining, and you're far in the backcountry, is no time or place to learn how a stove operates. So thoroughly read the owner's instruction booklet, then take the stove into your backyard and cook your lunch one sunny afternoon to learn exactly how everything works.

COMPARISONS OF POPULAR STOVES

Model	Weight (ozs.)	Weight with fuel	Height (in.)	Width/diam. (in.)	Length (in.)	Fuel used	Fuel capacity (ozs.)	Boiling time (min.)	Burning time (min.)	Pressure pump	Cold-weather use	Simplicity of operation
Bluet S-200	16	27	4½	3½	9½	Butane	6.3	5	190	No	Poor	High
Coleman Peak 1	31	41	6½	4½	–	White gas	10.0	3½	210	Yes	Yes	Average
EFI Mini	8	18	–	4½	1½	Propane	6.2	6	195	No	Poor	High
GAZ Globetrotter	10	16	5½	3½	–	Butane	6.0	7	70	No	Poor	High
Hank Roberts Mini	8	17	–	4½	1½	Propane	6.2	6	195	No	Fair	High
MSR Gasoline	16	32	3½	3¼	9½	White gas	16.0	4	130	Yes	Yes	Average
MSR Multi-Fuel	16	32	3½	3¼	9	Several	16.0	4	130	Yes	Yes	Average
Optimus 8R	23	26	3¼	5	5	White gas	3.2	7	70	No	Fair	Average
Optimus 77A	24	30	4½	8	–	Alcohol	6.0	7	25	No	Yes	High
Optimus 111	56	74	6	6	7	Kerosene	16.0	6	110	Yes	Yes	Average
Optimus 111B	56	74	4	6½	7	White gas	16.0	6	110	Yes	Yes	Average
Optimus 731	11	21	4	7	–	Propane	9.5	6	260	No	Yes	High
Phoebus 625	32	48	4½	3½	–	White gas	16.0	4	150	Yes	Yes	Average
Phoenix Mountaineer	32	48	7¼	5½	–	White gas	16.0	4½	190	Yes	Yes	Average
Svea 123R	18	22	5	4½	–	White gas	6.0	6	60	No	Fair	Average
Svea 123UR	12	22	5	4½	–	White gas	6.0	6	60	No	Fair	Average
Trangia 25	3.5	4.2	2	3	–	Alcohol	4.0	11½	45	No	Fair	High

- Owner's manuals packed with trail stoves are invaluable. Aside from general operating instructions, there is likely a trouble-shooting guide that may be helpful if something goes wrong. You'll also probably find an exploded-parts diagram keyed to serial numbers of various parts. This can be a lifesaver if you disassemble the stove, for cleaning, say, but forget exactly how it goes back together. The parts list can save a lot of time, too, if your stove malfunctions and you find yourself at a pay phone calling local outfitters to see which one stocks your stove's replacement parts. Take your owner's manual with you on outings, protected from moisture in a sealed, plastic sandwich bag.

- If your stove does not come with a small, all-purpose wrench, buy one from the manufacturer. It's handy for tightening various nuts or fixtures that may work loose with time.

- Invest in a special cleaning needle or wire made for cleaning out burner heads or fuel-tube orifices that sometimes become clogged with food drippings or carbon residue. To clean, unscrew the burner head and burner tip; otherwise, you'll only be pushing the congestion deeper into the tube, where it is sure to cause continued problems.

- When disassembling and cleaning your stove at home, use a small can of pressurized air to blow dust and other debris out of tiny places you can't reach with your fingers.

- Some stoves, such as those made by Optimus, can be equipped with an optional pressure pump that attaches to the fuel filler tube. This can make those particular models more efficient in cold weather.

Buy an extra burner key for your stove and keep it handy in case you lose the original. Keys that double as multi-fixture wrenches are recommended, since it may be necessary to tighten nuts and bolts on your stove occasionally.

A cleaning needle of the type shown here should be packed with your trail stove. Use it in the outback for emergency cleaning of burner jets or fuel-tube orifices that sometimes become clogged with carbon residue or food drippings.

Aerosol cans of pressurized, clean air are ideal for cleaning hard-to-reach places on trail stoves.

- While it is generally safe to cook in your tent with adequate ventilation, don't actually light your stove in the tent. There's just too much risk of a dangerous flare-up. Better to light the stove outside, then, with the flame low, carry it in.

- Sometimes, with some stoves, the hand pump suddenly stops pressurizing the fuel fount. Most likely, the problem can be remedied quickly. Remove the pump's integral rod assembly and you'll see a circular leather washer affixed to the end. This washer forces air into the stove's fuel tank, but if it has dried out pressure will escape. Massage the leather with your fingers for several minutes with several drops of oil to make the washer soft and pliable again. Use cooking oil if nothing else is handy.

- If your stove begins to burn with a high yellow flame when you first ignite it, the burner tube has not become sufficiently warmed to vaporize the fuel. Remedy this by turning down the burner dial to a very small flame until it turns blue-white and you can hear a faint roaring sound.

- With a propane or butane stove, be very careful when installing a fresh fuel cartridge so you don't strip the soft threads at the mouth of the bottle. If you suspect a leak, test the area with a little soapy water to see if bubbles pop up. Never use a match!

- In cold weather, the efficiency of a propane or butane stove can be improved by keeping the fuel cartridge as warm as possible (but never so warm you can't hold it in your bare hands). One way of doing this is by keeping the bottle in your coat pocket or close to your body. But when actually cooking, place a sheet of aluminum foil around the base of the stove so that heat from the burner reflects in the direction of the fuel canister. This is en-

Stoves that use pump-plunger assemblies may in time cease to hold pressure. The problem is that the small, circular leather washer at the end of the plunger has dried out. You can easily remove the plunger, rub oil into the leather with your fingertips until it is soft and pliable, and reinstall it.

Some types of trail stoves use generators that occasionally become clogged and must be replaced. Simply use a wrench to remove the old generator and then slip in the new one.

tirely safe — these stoves are engineered so that no heat at all is ordinarily conducted from the stove to the fuel bottle.

- As a propane or butane canister gradually becomes depleted, the pressure inside the can greatly diminishes. As a result, it may take three times as long to boil water with a canister that is almost empty, compared to one that is full. There is no solution, but good advice is never to embark on a new outing with only a partially used fuel canister. Carry a fresh one to serve as a spare.

10

Tools of the Trail

My first trail-cooking equipment was a dusty cast-iron skillet I'd found in the basement, a three-pound lard can fitted with a wire bail, and a one-pound syrup can transformed into a makeshift coffee pot. I scrounged and haphazardly assembled them amidst heady thoughts of early pioneers, Indian scouts, and buffalo hunters. Adventure beckoned.

Of course, at age eleven I was not yet drinking "java," and so had no pressing need for a coffee pot, but, like many impressionable youngsters, I found my inner passion for trail cooking stirred by exciting novels of the time such as *West of the Pecos, The Cimarron Trail,* and *The Muleskinner.* I figured if a frypan, stew kettle, and coffee pot were always in the saddlebags of the likes of Jim Bridger, Buffalo Bill Cody, and Kit Carson, then they'd accompany me, too.

It was about the time both tin cans burned through the bottom (the "coffee pot" having been especially well-used in brewing dozens of gallons of hot chocolate) that I found myself involved in Boy Scouts and shortly thereafter introduced to a whole new world of outdoor cooking. To my ecstatic pleasure, we actually hiked deep into woodland regions to practice our craft. (Until I became a full-fledged Scout, Mom had decreed that my "pioneering" would not transcend the perimeter of our large backyard; fortunately an abundance of trees and shrubs, along with a very vivid imagination, made this restriction relatively easy to cope with.) Scouting was also responsible for bringing to my attention the lightweight realm of aluminum.

During the last twenty-five years little has changed — I find the miracle metal made from bauxite ore still dominates the field of trail-cooking gear. As any knowledgeable chef will affirm, aluminum is not the most ideal material for cooking — cast iron is at the top of the list, followed by copper-clad stainless steel, both too heavy for most trail uses — but it is the best alternative for those who must shoulder bedrolls, housing, provisions, and "kitchens" when far from bright city lights. Therefore, the vast majority of cooking gear you'll find these days is made from aluminum.

The kinds of trail utensils you'll need depend on your food preferences, cooking methods compatible with them, number of people in the party, and many other variables. Nonetheless, after many years of roaming around in virtually every state and Canadian province, I have certain ideas about what works best "for most people most of the time." So let's look at the most common items of cooking and eating equipment in the hopes that beginning trail trampers will see greater success in properly outfitting themselves. Old-timers may learn a new trick or two, as well.

POTS AND PANS

The heart of any cooking-gear assemblage is the venerable frying pan. If it is a deep-dish variety with high sloping sides, you can make your morning's bacon and eggs, soup for lunch, a casserole for dinner, bread anytime (by filling the pan with dough and tipping it up at a sharp angle before a fire), even coffee — anything that needs to be fried, baked, boiled, poached, slowly simmered, or merely warmed.

To be sure, most outdoor cooks want to have along additional, more specialized implements, but if for some reason I were restricted to only one, a high-walled skillet would be

These anglers are making good use of their trusty skillet to fry some fresh fish.

it. Among other tasks routinely taken on by frying pans are shaving, washing out socks, soaking tired feet, and swatting bugs that crawl into the tent at night. It is one piece of equipment that literally does it all.

I prefer a 9½-inch frypan because this size is just right for two people, yet still easy to pack. If you're cooking only for yourself, or going ultralight, an 8-inch pan will suffice. Or, if your menu for a brief one- or two-day outing allows, even one of the tiny lids that house your trail stove may be adequate. If more than two members are in the party, there is the tendency to want to lug along a frypan much larger than the traditional 9½-inch size. I'll give this a quick thumbs-down any day: much better to opt for two, smaller size skillets than one jumbo model.

When selecting one or more skillets it's worth the extra dollar or two to invest in those with a nonstick coating such as Teflon or Silverstone. The dividends: easy clean-up, less chance of burned food, and you don't have to pack along or use nearly as much cooking oil.

When shopping for a skillet, also pay careful attention to the handle. This is a critical area of any frypan's construction because more than one famished soul has experienced the maddening frustration of having his skillet and handle separate at some inopportune moment. I like frypans with handles rigidly and permanently attached, but there are situations in which these are too unwieldy to stow in one's pack. Then there is no choice but to use a model with a handle that folds downward under the pan and out of the way, swings sharply to one side, or detaches altogether by means of a slot-and-tongue arrangement.

The time-tested Army mess kit, still available in military-surplus stores, is a splendid example of worryfree construction with its hinged handle permanently attached to a deep, oblong-shaped skillet and mated, partitioned lid that doubles as a plate. When nested together, there is enough room

The heart of all camp-cooking gear is the frypan. Best type for trail cooking is 9½ inches in diameter, of deep-dish design, with a sturdy handle. Shown here are two Palco models, both of aluminum; one at right has Teflon coating.

The time-tested Army mess kit, still available in Army surplus stores, suits the needs of many backpackers.

When opened, the Army mess kit reveals an oval frypan with sturdy handle and a compartmented plate. There is enough room inside to house silverware and other essentials.

Frying-pan handle designs vary. The author favors the tongue-and-slot handle shown here, but those which fold to one side for easy packing are also durable.

inside for utensils and a few other odds and ends. An almost carbon copy of this handy contraption is the Boy Scout mess kit, which is a few ounces lighter in weight but suffers from a swing-away handle that must be alternately loosened or tightened with a bolt and wing nut; Murphy's Law states you will lose no less than twenty-seven of these bolt-nut affairs over any given five-year period.

In the pot or kettle category, there are at least several dozen designs to choose from. Again, a good rule of thumb is to decide in favor of several smaller vessels rather than one gargantuan model. For a meal no more posh than a one-person sheepherder's stew, you may be able to get by with the lower half of your backpack stove case. At the other extreme, anything larger than a 6-quart kettle probably will be a hindrance more than a help, unless there are several pals along and everyone is willing to share the hefty gear. Other justification for oversize cooking vessels may come into play if a canoe, Jeep, or packhorse is summoned for at least a portion of the journey.

Nested cooking kits are extremely popular because everything is housed in a single unit. Marianne Weiss shows a large kit capable of serving six and a lightweight two-person model.

Most pots and kettles for outdoor cooking have no handles on their sides but instead are fitted with heavy-duty wire bails on top so that removing cookware from a fire leaves hands as far away from the flames as possible.

The Mirro Cookware Company and Palco Products are two major producers of trail-cooking equipment that, in addition to skillets, offer pots and kettles coated on their inner surfaces with smooth, nonstick surfaces like Teflon. By all means, seriously consider these vessels if your menus frequently include casseroles, stews, and dishes such as spaghetti or macaroni and cheese. Otherwise, resign yourself to spending extra time diligently scraping and chipping crusted food remnants with your pocketknife. Your food will cook more quickly and not be diluted by raindrops if you buy lightweight lids for your pots and pans.

Without a doubt one of the greatest boons to outdoor cooking are the nested kits that are so popular these days.

154

They are far more convenient and pleasurable to use than a random collection of pots and pans purchased separately and then packed willy-nilly.

A typical nested cooking kit consists of a bottom pot covered with a lid that, when a separate handle is attached, serves as a frypan. Inside are graduated sizes of still other pots and pans and even a small percolator (in all but the scaled-down, ultralight backpack models). You'll also find four or six dinner plates, a corresponding number of cups, assorted lids for the vessels, and just enough additional room between the components for miscellaneous items such as tea bags, packets of instant coffee, and clean-up supplies. These nested cooking kits range in size from one-person models to those capable of serving as many as six.

Large, nested cook kits provide everything necessary to prepare sumptuous meals. Note the heavy wire bail handles on the pots and the nesting arrangement of the cups.

Their main advantage is that all the cooking gear remains together in a single, compact unit.

I'd also advise making or buying some type of stuff bag with a drawstring closure for your cooking kit. The strategy here is *not* to provide the cooking kit with special protection, but to safeguard clothing and other gear from it. Hurry-up meals and rushed clean-up operations due to rain or the anxious urge to get back to the fishing periodically happen, and a nylon or denim carrying bag for the cooking gear will prevent some overlooked grease spot or black carbon smudge from streaking something it shouldn't.

DISHES AND CUPS

I have not yet found campware dishes to my liking. Maybe I'm too fussy, but it seems there are only two kinds available and both have drawbacks.

The aluminum ones are lightweight, stack easily for convenient storage in cooking kits, are easy to clean, and are virtually indestructible, but aluminum is either very hot or gruesomely cold. Food that is not piping hot when placed upon the metal tends to lose heat faster than it ordinarily would because of the nature of the aluminum. And few things are more unpalatable than congealed gravy or cold eggs. On the other hand, extremely hot food taken from the skillet and immediately placed on an aluminum plate will burn the recipient's fingers.

Plastic plates, whether sectioned or flat, are not much better. Although they too nest well, are even lighter in weight than aluminum, and—an added plus—hold heat much longer without searing one's flesh, they are made of

The main problem with aluminum cookwear is the gray layer of oxidation that accumulates over a period of time. It is harmless but unappealing and makes gear look dirty. Remove the dingy coating once a year by scrubbing with detergent and steel wool.

very soft plastics, which are susceptible to superficial scratches and knife cuts during the course of eating. In little time, these slices in the plastic take on food stains that are impossible to remove. After only a dozen meals, the dishes often appear so unsightly you may feel you're eating from dirty plates, which does nothing to enhance one's appetite. Plastic plates also become smudged with an oxidation residue from being in contact with the aluminum pots and pans during storage and transportation, and no amount of scrubbing will entirely remove the displeasing (but harmless) gray matter.

Plastic plates and cups versus aluminum: Both are lightweight, but both have drawbacks. Plastic doesn't withstand the rigors of repeated use and aluminum is either very hot or gruesomely cold.

This two-person nested cook kit includes two plates, two cups, a frypan, and a kettle—yet weighs only 13 ounces.

One alternative to the use of plates, especially if you frequently have "soupy" meals like casseroles and stews, are thick plastic bowls with sides that slant outward sharply. I'm thinking mainly of the kind you get for free when buying 1- and 2-pound tubs of margarine at the grocery store.

These clever little all-purpose vessels can be used for mixing ingredients as well as eating, and thereby eliminate the need for a wider assortment of cooking gear. For example, reconstitute your breakfast eggs in such a bowl, pour them into your skillet, and as they are cooking rinse the bowl and use it to eat your dry cereal and milk. Then rinse the bowl again and now eat your finished eggs. Rinse the bowl again, mix your pancake batter, pour it into the frypan, rinse the bowl yet once more, and then fill it with the 'cakes and syrup. On go-light trips this mixing-rinsing-eating operation can be honed to perfection for each and every meal using countless variations of foods, and when each meal is concluded there is only one dish and the frypan to wash and pack away.

Plastic versus metal cups have the same advantages and disadvantages as those found in plateware. If it's a midsummer outing and all you'll be drinking are cold beverages, nothing can surpass the internationally popular Sierra cup made from spun aluminum. It seems almost like a standard fixture on the outside of packframes, where it's always handy. Yet on a cold-weather outing, mix instant tea, coffee, or a dry soup mix in your Sierra cup, and the metal is almost certain to burn your lips. A plastic cup keeps beverages hot much longer, with little risk of self-cremation, but soon the thing may look so stained and unappetizing you'll not want to drink from it.

This is one arena in which cookware companies need to put their research-and-development folks to work. Some type of super-hard finish on plastic plates and cups may be the answer.

UTENSILS

Every member of a hunting or fishing party should have his own personal eating utensils, that he alone is responsible for, and knows the whereabouts of. Nothing is more inappropriate to efficient traveling, trail-cooking logistics, and individual temeraments than a hodgepodge of mismatched knives, forks, and spoons cluttering the bottom of someone's pack, perhaps puncturing food bags or raingear, and jingle-jangling with each step forward.

I personally have a fetish for mated eating utensils in which knife, fork, and spoon remain attached to each other by means of a slip-lock rivet (no parts to lose), yet can be separated the instant the food is served. After eating, the three are reunited and slipped into a vinyl carrying case to prevent sharp edges or protrusions from gouging other gear.

However, this is my own preference and certainly not the final word. Many 'packers prefer, instead, a versatile Swiss Army Knife with utensils and sundry other tools that swing out of the knife's familiar red case. One inventive chap I know even went as far as to design his own combination fork-spoon by cutting off the handle of a fork and soldering the tine section to the end of his spoon handle. He needs no dinner knife as he always has his sheath blade or pocket-knife along.

Even though each camper assumes the responsibility for his or her personal eating utensils, it's still necessary to have a small set of communal cooking tools for use around stove or fire. A spatula heads the list, followed by some type of large spoon and long-handled fork. However, keep in mind if you're using cooking gear coated with Teflon it is imperative to use utensils made of nylon or hard plastic. Teflon and similar slick surfaces are incredibly easy to scratch with metal utensils, and resulting bare spots will cause food there to burn and stick.

Each trail tramper should have his own personal eating gear, such as the handy knife-fork-spoon arrangement that fits together with slots and rivets. There also should be a community set of utensils for cooking. Make a storage bag for them from discarded denim.

From a discarded pair of old denim jeans, it's no complex chore to sew together a modest carrying case for these utensils. A wrap-around cord ties them into a neat little bundle.

Few trail cooks use traditional cloth potholders nowadays. They prefer to pick up hot pots or pans or arrange them around a fire with squeeze-type pot clamps that look almost like pliers. Several lightweight varieties are on the market, none costing more than a couple of bucks.

Some provision has to be made for measuring various ingredients to concoct certain recipes. For small quantities, I use a tiny plastic measuring spoon only 4 inches long. One

Extremely handy around the fire or campstove is a gadget that resembles pliers and takes the place of a cloth potholder. It grabs canned goods or utensils that don't have handles and prevents burned fingers.

end holds ½ teaspoon, the other end ⅓ teaspoon. With these two fractional amounts it is possible to measure out very closely ¼ teaspoon, 1 teaspoon, 1 tablespoon, ⅔ teaspoon, and the other most commonly used amounts simply by filling each receptacle as many times as needed.

A measuring cup of sorts would come in handy, but its infrequent use would constitute excess baggage. My solution is to take a metal-etching scribe and mark the inside of my Sierra drinking cup with gradation lines. Do this at home by filling a standard measuring cup ⅓ full of water, then pouring the water into the Sierra cup and marking the water level. After that, appropriately mark other common liquid measures.

MAKESHIFT COOKING IMPLEMENTS

A rapid glance through a Boy Scout Handbook or any survival manual reveals untold numbers of cooking tricks. They range in ingenuity from simple dingle sticks to support pots over a fire, to revolving meat spits and elaborate grillworks woven from green willow branches. I have seen instructions for baking fish in clay, steaming gamebirds in green thistlesnicker leaves, frying eggs on flat rocks heated by coals, boiling water in a brown paper bag, and even drawings showing in intimate detail how to build complicated underground networks of rock-lined chambers for baking this or smoking that.

In truth, the great majority of these gimmicks are enormously time consuming and highly dependent on hard-to-find but strategic materials. Worse, for the most part, they either don't work, are highly impractical, or result in meals that are disappointing, at best.

I remember once catching a brace of beautiful smallmouth bass while camping along the shore of a remote lake in upper Wisconsin, and relishing the thought of their succulent tenderness. In a moment of slack mental deficiency I decided to broil them on a grill I had read about in a leading outdoor magazine, that could cunningly be made of intertwined birch whips.

I followed the directions to the letter—for three hours. (I would have been better off doing more fishing.) The fish were almost done when suddenly one small and seemingly innocent part of the grillwork burned through, causing the rest of the structure to collapse, depositing my meal in the soot and ashes. After regaining my composure, I went fishing again, luckily caught two more bass, and this time entrusted them to my aluminum frypan.

Perhaps others are more successful at such endeavors. But in my mind life is too short, and high-quality cooking

Baking bread on a stick is quick and easy, not to mention creative.

implements too convenient, to risk the mental torment of losing one's well-deserved dinner at the end of a long, hard day.

One failsafe exception even I will attempt, however, is baking bread on a stick. My favorite is bannock, the bread seventeenth-century French-Canadian voyagers heavily relied upon when establishing trading and trapping routes in northern Quebec and Ontario. The dough—enough for two portions — consists of 2 cups of flour, $\frac{1}{2}$ teaspoon salt, 4 tablespoons powdered milk, and 2 teaspoons baking powder.

Mix all the dry ingredients at home and place them in a plastic bag. In camp, add just enough water to make a stiff, somewhat sticky dough. With your hands, press the dough out flat on a sheet of aluminum foil until it is about 1 inch thick, then cut it into 1-inch-wide strips with your knife. Next, wrap the strips in spiraling fashion around a green hardwood limb that has had the bark removed. The stickiness of the dough, combined with judicial pinching here and there, will hold it in place. Then simply suspend the works over a bed of coals, turning it frequently until the dough puffs up and turns golden brown. Just break off big pieces and smear them with butter or jam, or use them to mop your plate.

In the absence of a potholder or pot grabber, a makeshift implement can be whittled from a 4-inch-long branch from a softwood. Remove the bark, then cut a lengthwise slice that goes almost, but not all the way, through the wood and leaves a type of hinge. Place the slot over the wire bail of a pot and squeeze. You should be able to lift it without burning your fingers. Similarly, a forked stick with a prong whittled out, as shown in the accompanying illustration, can be used to pour hot liquids from a pot.

If you prefer not to pack a long-handled fork, a makeshift two-tined invention can quickly be made in camp from a 3-foot-long green branch that is forked at one end and duly sharpened. A similar tool can be contrived to serve as a rake for use with a keyhole fire (see Chapter 8), or occasionally pushing coals around in the cooking pit.

From time to time I have also used coat hangers in various ways. With a pair of pliers that have side-cutters in their

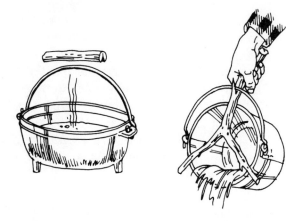

A 1-inch-diameter stick split lengthwise, with the green bark acting as a hinge, can be used to lift hot pots from a fire. A forked stick cut like a slingshot, with a notch whittled in the handle, can be used to pour hot soup, beverages, or stew.

jaws, the hangers can be bent into numerous shapes. One word of caution: Coat-hanger wire is not very strong and not well suited to heavy-duty use. But when lightweight, one-person cooking chores are in order, you can fold a coat hanger over on itself for a makeshift grill that will support a small frypan or soup pot. You can even make a pot or frypan by fashioning the framework from the wire and covering it with heavy-duty foil. Don't get delusions of grandeur, however: the pot should be trusted with no more than 1 cup of liquid, and the frypan suitable only for things like a single egg, a few sausage links, or perhaps a small trout. Assorted utensils can also be fashioned easily from coat-hanger wire, including an extension handle for a tiny frypan.

Aluminum foil, in addition to being used as described above, is handy around camp for other chores as well. To

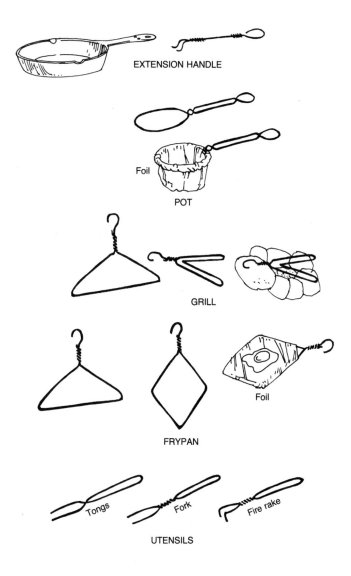

EXTENSION HANDLE

Foil

POT

GRILL

FRYPAN

Foil

Tongs   Fork   Fire rake

UTENSILS

Coat-hanger tools are easy to fashion in camp. Using only your hands or pliers, you can make implements like the ones shown here. Just remember that coat-hanger wire is too flimsy for heavy-duty chores.

save weight and space, remove it from its box, strip about 10 yards and fold it into a small packet. (In Chapter 12, I'll describe how to make a reflector oven from foil — no gimmick, I assure you.) One-pot dishes feature fish, gamebirds, small game, big game, or pork, sausage, chicken, beef or hamburger.

You can use heavy-duty foil for this, or a double wrapping of lightweight aluminum. Some claim the heavy stuff is more durable. I personally prefer two layers of the lightweight. The essence of foil cooking is trapping heat, steam, and juices inside a tightly sealed envelope; this cooks the food without its burning or sticking to the housing. Should a heavy-foil wrapping inadvertently receive a puncture, or even a pinhole leak, the steam will escape and the food is likely to scorch. A double wrapping of lightweight foil guards against this. Also, when the food has cooked and been extracted from the fire, you can peel away the outer, soot-covered wrapper, turn back the edges of the inner foil pouch and eat right from the makeshift plate.

To prepare your meal, spread out a 14-inch square of foil, be it a single or double layer. In the middle lay approximately ¾ pound of the meat of your choice. Add sliced potatoes, cheese if you like, and one or more types of vegetables (even freeze-dried or dehydrated varieties that have soaked five minutes in water but have not been cooked). Sprinkle in a dash of salt, pepper, and spices appropriate to the meal. Then cup the foil slightly and add about ¼ cup of water. Finally, bring up the sides of the foil the remainder of the way and fold and pinch them together so they will hold steam. I like to set these little dinners right on top of the coals for about twenty minutes, then turn them over to cook a while on the other side. Others simply bury them deep in the middle of the bed of coals for the duration of the cooking.

There is no way to judge precisely the required cooking

time of foods in foil; it rests largely with the thickness of the meat being used. For most meat and potato dishes, however, forty minutes is a good guideline. If the food is not done after forty minutes, you can always wrap it up tightly again and put it on the coals for another fifteen minutes. Conversely, the protective nature of the foil will prevent thoroughly cooked food from burning for at least a short while if it is not immediately removed from the fire.

11

Food Storage in Camp

Across outdoor America reside zillions of raccoons, skunks, opossums, porcupines, crows, magpies, and assorted other small critters that will gladly, at any opportunity, try to relieve campers of their larder. Their conniving and trickery knows no bounds. They'll skulk about in the dead of night, trying to home-in upon the source of some delectable odor while simultaneously planning a secret raid. Or they'll wait until you're just barely out of sight of camp, picking berries or looking for deer tracks, then brazenly chart a nonstop course for your pack or tent. Even chipmunks and field mice can be pesky nuisances (their favorite foods are seeds, nuts, and salt, so your bags of trail snacks are extremely high on their hit list).

Now and then there also may be problems with the bigger beasties such as wolverines, wolves, or coyotes. But of paramount importance and concern are bears; many times they engage in sneak tactics but other times, especially in national parks where they have become accustomed to handouts, simply stroll into camp and take what they want.

If a bear's keen nose captures the fragrant whiff of a pan of lasagna left over from dinner, a freeze-dried bacon bar, or a bag of chocolate-chip cookies, and those toothsome delights happen to be in your tent, count upon the bruin just inviting himself to supper. Like a true gentleman he'll enter through the front door, but finding you at home promptly exit through the nearest wall, taking with him ragged canvas, tent stakes, guy ropes, and perhaps a piece of your hide.

Every trailman should know fundamental ways of safeguarding his rations from these thieves (and in so doing lessen any risks to his own invaluable carcass). Freeze-dried and dehydrated backpack foods require no preservation, but there will be times when knowing how to keep foods cold or warm — and, at the same time, safe — can be crucial. When you've caught fish along the way and want to save them for the next day's breakfast, for instance, you've got to stash them where they won't fall into the wrong hands (or paws).

HANG IT HIGH

The most effective method of protecting food from creature attacks is to place it high out of their reach. This means wrapping the food properly, then hanging it in a tree.

In my pack, I like to have all of my food in a single, large, heavy-duty plastic bag, tied at the neck with a string closure. This makes it easy, when I settle into a campsite at the end of the day, to extract the plastic bag, tie a lightweight cord to the neck, throw the rope over a high limb, and hoist 'er aloft. The plastic bag also protects your food from rain or snow. If you use your pack as a repository for assorted bags of food tucked here and there, you'll have to lift the entire pack off the ground. And just as you get the thing up in the air and squared away for the night — you guessed it — you'll remember the bug dope, candle lantern, or some other essential still packed away.

Hanging your food bag from a sturdy limb high out of reach will foil the attempts of pesky raccoons and bears.

172

When trees do not have long, stout limbs, string a running line from one tree trunk to another, then suspend your food bag from the middle of the line.

If bears are in the region, your food bag should be about 12 feet above the ground. If none are around, 8 feet is sufficient. Remember that bears, raccoons, and many other animals are outstanding climbers and have amazing manual dexterity. So suspend your food bag in such a way that they cannot reach it by climbing adjacent tree trunks or hanging onto a limb with one hand and making a long reach with the other.

If the tree branches around your camp are not long and stout enough to support a food bag away from the tree trunk — let's say the trees are mostly pines and firs — you'll have to string a high line from one trunk to another, then hang the food bag in the middle with a second line the same way you'd throw it over a tree limb.

Three long poles lashed together at the apex to form a tripod is another solution. The food bag then hangs from a rope tied to the peak of the tripod, so it is at least 6 feet above the ground. However, this gambit is to be used only when small critters are a nuisance, never in bear country. The bruins will merely knock the whole thing down.

Suppose you are above timberline, or in muskeg country in the far north where there are no trees, or in the arid land

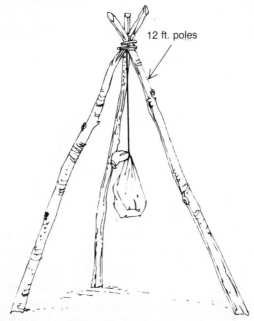

12 ft. poles

A tripod food cache is effective against field mice and other small animals. Don't use it in bear country, though; the bruins will merely knock it over.

of the desert Southwest and the poor excuses for trees are spindly little bushes. In cases like these, there's no way to place your food high out of the reach of animal robbers, but you do have other recourses. One is setting your food bag on the ground and then covering it with some article of clothing. I like to use a T-shirt that has been "fermenting" in my dirty-laundry bag. Usually, the strong human scent will ward away all but the most desperate wildlife species.

Another ploy is to set your food bag on the ground and sprinkle some little nicotine sulfate crystals in a circle around it. This is a well-known animal repellent often used around vegetable gardens and shrubbery. It is sold in most pet stores and garden shops, will not kill plantlife, and is harmless to pets and wild animals but has an odor they do not like and will avoid. Moth balls or moth flakes will keep them away, too. All three of these items are inexpensive, and a couple of 35mm film canisters filled with one potion or another weigh only a few ounces in your pack.

Porcupines can be a terrible problem in many areas of the country. In addition to making assaults on a 'packer's food cache, the critters have an insatiable love for salt and will gnaw on virtually anything with traces of perspiration on it—axe handles, knife handles, canoe paddles, gunstocks, shoulder harnesses of knapsacks, cloth coverings of canteens and countless other items. I know one guy who discovered one of his hiking boots, left outside at night, with an entire side chewed apart. Always keep personal clothing inside the tent at night, or, in the case of very tiny tents, hang your pack from a high tree limb.

Safeguarding other gear such as canoe paddles and axes from porcupines can tax anyone's ingenuity. In most circumstances, the best bet is probably to use lengths of lightweight string or cord to suspend the equipment from tree branches at least 4 feet above the ground.

A menace in the semitropical regions of the South and Southeast is ants, but they are easy to deal with. If you know in advance ants are likely to be a problem, you can fashion an antproof "hook" at home. Take a short, wide-mouth tin can such as the type tuna is packed in, and wash it clean. Punch or drill a small hole in the bottom, then insert a 12-inch length of coat-hanger wire through the hole and solder it in place. Finally, with pliers, bend each end of the wire into a hook shape. In camp, tie a length of cord to one end of the hook and throw the rope over a tree branch. Now tie another shorter length of rope to the other hook,

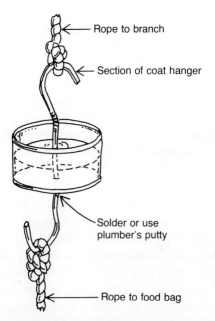

Rope to branch

Section of coat hanger

Solder or use plumber's putty

Rope to food bag

An antproof hook can easily be made at home from a tin can for use in hot climates where crawling bugs are a problem.

and to that tie your food bag so that it hangs a few feet above the ground. Fill the can with water, and you'll have no ants in your food. Even if they manage to climb from the tree branch down the length of rope, they can go no farther when they reach the can because of the water. Regardless of the thievery-prevention device you use, make sure your food cache is at least 50 yards away from your immediate campsite. That way, you're not likely to have a face-to-face confrontation with a furry intruder. Likewise, wash dirty dishes and cooking implements after each meal; never let them accumulate around the campsite. Candy bars and other late-night snacks in your tent are equally verboten. If you want some type of food to raise your blood-sugar level or help your body produce heat during the night, eat before retiring, and do it outside your sleeping quarters.

KEEPING IT COLD

In winter or any other time the temperature dips below 38° F, there is little need to worry about food preservation in camp or on the trail. But I would suggest foods in your pack that require cold be placed toward the rear (away from your back) so your body heat has no effect on them. Other times of year at altitudes above 6,000 feet, you're likely to chance upon the remains of snowbanks, ideal for the temporary storage of wild greens you have gathered, freshly caught fish, game meats, or other meats brought from home. Southeast facing slopes do not receive the same intense sunlight or winds as those facing northwest and therefore are where snowbanks are likely to remain the longest. But small remnants of snow and ice patches may be found in other places, as well, if the terrain is shaded most of the day or in the lee of high rock walls.

One way to keep perishables cool in hot weather is to place them in a watertight plastic bag, add a rock for weight, then submerge the works in a cold stream or spring. Here the author stores ruffed grouse in a cool pool on his Ohio game preserve.

Throughout other regions of the country, heed the advice given earlier: Begin your trek with perishable foods either frozen or very well chilled and wrapped in newspaper, and plan to eat them within forty-eight hours.

In very hot climates, it's often possible to contrive some sort of refrigerator in camp. Nothing fancy mind you, just a

2-foot-deep hole dug into the earth to reach cool soil. Do this in a shady location, then cover your plastic bag with damp moss, leaves, or slabs of old bark peeled from a downed tree. Your food will not become as cold as it would in a real refrigerator, but it will be as much as 25 degrees cooler than the air temperature, and that will likely get you by for a day or so.

There are two other methods of keeping food cold that perhaps are even more convenient. One is to wrap the perishables carefully in a waterproof plastic bag and submerge it in a cold stream. A rock inside the bag will hold it down, and a cord tied around the neck and then to some shoreline object will prevent the current from carrying it away. If you can find a natural spring, that's even better. Search the V-notch area where two sharply sloping hillsides come together; wherever the vegetation is thick and green you'll probably find a spring. All that's necessary then is to dig down into the moist earth with your hands. If water begins to trickle slowly into the hole the spring is confirmed, and often it will be so icy cold it will make your hands numb.

Finally, there is an Arizona guide named Mickey Thomas who long ago taught me the trick of using evaporation as a means of cooling foods. He always had along a small cloth sack made of muslin or burlap. Inside he placed his plastic bag of perishables, then hung the sack from a tree branch and thoroughly soaked the fabric with water. Breezes caused the water to evaporate and rendered a cooling effect. Usually, the bag had to be resoaked every two or three hours, depending upon the temperature.

This cooling-by-evaporation phenomenon, in fact, is the reason many Western-style canteens have blanket coverings. The blanket material is thick and holds water like a sponge. Just soak it now and then, let nature take its course, and you're always assured a cool drink.

Another way to cool foods in camp is to place them in a burlap or muslin bag, hang it from a tree branch, then douse the outside with water. Even in warm weather, breezes cause the water to evaporate and cool the contents.

In cold weather, one way to prevent foods from freezing is to dig a 2-foot-deep hole in the earth, place your food bag in the bottom, then cover it with leaves, grass, or slabs of bark from dead trees.

KEEPING IT WARM

In most outdoor ramblings it's not really necessary to keep foods warm, but sometimes you do have to prevent them from freezing. In your pack, place those particular foods or liquids as close to your back as possible. And when you climb out of your pack harness for a rest break, set your gear in direct sunlight.

181

Around camp, avoid storing grub in shaded areas. Subject it to as much radiant heat from bright light as possible. In bitter-cold weather, a good trick it to dig a 2-foot-deep hole in the earth, set your food in the bottom, then cover it with leaves or bark. Just as the earth acts as an insulator to keep food cool in summer, it works just the opposite way to keep it warm in winter.

When you hang food in a tree to safeguard it from animals in winter, use a heavy-duty, black plastic bag, which will absorb every possible smidgen of sunlight and heat rather than reflect it.

The savvy sportsman preplans outings and related meals to avoid food-preservation problems. However, if and when they arise, the common-sense solutions described here should be entirely adequate for brief periods.

STORING GAME MEAT, BIRDS, AND FISH

I remember one packtrip into the Bob Marshall Wilderness during mid-July when we constantly mopped our foreheads as we pushed on through blistering 90° heat to a secluded alpine lake in the high country. It was a unique experience to be wearing hiking shorts and lightweight shirts, yet seeing swatches of snow here and there left over from a late spring thaw. We caught fish for dinner, and merely jabbed them into a snowbank underneath a rock overhang to keep them cold. Nothing but the tails were allowed to stick out of the snow, to mark their locations, and despite the warm air temperature those trout were as icy cold, half a day later, as if they had been in a deep freeze.

Another way to preserve fish is simply to keep them alive as long as possible by securing them to a cord stringer. Or kill them, promptly remove their insides, and bury them in a thick blanket of wet moss, ferns, or leaves. You can also

When the weather is warm, remove the insulating hides of big-game animals as quickly as possible. Then, to discourage insects, slip a muslin game bag around the carcass.

place them in a plastic bag and submerge them in a cold stream or spring.

Gamebirds and small game animals can be kept cool in much the same way as fish, but since they are surrounded by insulation in the form of fur or feathers, remove these to allow the meat to cool as quickly as possible. I once kept two jackrabbits cool by first skinning them, then placing them in plastic bags, and next slipping them into a pair of thick wool hunting socks, which I hung from a tree limb and regularly soaked with water.

Larger game animals are somewhat difficult to handle, but happily the seasons for them are usually cool, if not downright cold. Again, remove the thick insulating hide and get the carcass off the ground so there is as much free circulation of air as possible. To guard against flies, birds or insects, enclose the carcass in a muslin game bag made for that purpose. Usually the night hours will be cold enough to chill the meat thoroughly. The following morning, wrap the carcass with a tarp or even in your sleeping bag (still in the muslin sack, of course) to keep the meat cool during the sunny daylight hours. In warmer temperatures, quartering the meat will speed the cooling effect. Move the individual pieces as necessary so they remain well shaded.

With any fish, birds, or game meats, follow the other precautions outlined earlier, such as draping an article of your clothing over the meat, hanging it high out of the reach of animals, or sprinkling nicotine sulfate crystals around the cache.

▴▴ 12 ▴▴▴▴▴▴▴▴▴▴▴▴▴▴▴▴▴▴▴▴

Reflector-Oven Cooking

Tom Baker, the lucky fool, got his deer on opening day — during the first fifteen minutes of the season, no less. We were just 100 miles west of Denver, and Tom was hiking from camp to his blind when the buck, a big muley, jumped from tall sagebrush and bounded across the trail in front of him. Baker dropped the deer then and there.

The whole thing couldn't have turned out better. It was lucky for Tom, as I said, and for the rest of us in the group, as well. With his tag filled, Tom automatically became quartermaster of the firewood, chief water hauler, and full-time camp cook. And Tom Baker is the type of camp cook any hunting party would consider itself fortunate to have along.

Take what happened on the second day of our week-long hunt in the high country. Just as we were leaving camp early in the morning, I saw Tom busily gathering a dozen or so green sticks. At first I thought he was planning to heat some dishwater, or maybe take a bath. But he wouldn't be using green wood to burn a fire.

As it turned out, Tom was making a reflector oven. As he later explained, he lashed the green sticks together with a small spool of lightweight wire. The odd-looking framework of sticks then assembled, he next covered all sides but the front with aluminum foil. The result: a handily contrived reflector oven that took only half an hour to make but would last for the rest of our stay in the mountains.

Later that evening, we had two dozen of the best steaming-hot biscuits I ever ate, the perfect complement to a robust sheepherder's stew. For dessert, Baker produced two apple pies he had also made that day while we were hunting.

"I made up some dough, too," Tom said nonchalantly, "for hot cinnamon rolls for breakfast."

"I hope you're the first to get your deer again next year," one hunter told him.

That was my introduction to reflector-oven cooking. In the many years since, there have been few camps in which I haven't made use of this ingenious device. A reflector oven won't perform every kitchen duty, but it really shines (literally) when it comes to baking any kind of meat, fish, or fowl, and especially bread products. Any of these items are sure to be welcome surprises to any camp menu that otherwise may prove tiring and uneventful with its on-going emphasis on freeze-dried, boiled, or fried foods.

OVENS TO BUY OR MAKE

Hunters and other outdoorsmen can make use of three basic types of reflector ovens, depending upon how much gear they're able to pack along or other camp logistics: manufactured ones, makeshift models, and "quickie" affairs.

Manufactured ovens. When weight is not a crucial factor, I recommend one of the commercially manufactured reflector ovens. They are made of highly polished aluminum sheet metal in a one-piece, hinged assembly, so there is no chance of parts becoming lost. For easy portability, the hinged construction also allows the oven to be collapsed into a flat, folded unit that measures about 12 inches square by ½ inch thick. Mine weighs about 1½ pounds.

Several brands of reflector ovens are listed in the more complete camping mail-order catalogs. They're also available through some of the better backpacking shops, and are carried by retail stores that stock Boy Scout equipment. Prices are low, and the model of your choice, given a modicum of care, should last a lifetime.

Oven care. What is critical is that the high gloss of the oven's canted metal walls be preserved if the oven is to remain effective. I ruined the first oven I owned by scouring it with an abrasive cleanser, which dulled the polished

When weight is not a crucial factor, a factory-made reflector oven saves time. This one weighs only 1½ pounds and folds up for easy storage and transportation.

sheen of the aluminum. If drippings or food splatterings begin to accumulate, use the tip of your knife to remove them very gently, being careful not to gouge the metal. Never use a steel-wool pad or gritty detergent; they are sure to scratch and dull the soft metal surfaces of the oven. When complete washing does become necessary to remove grease and grime, use a mild liquid soap in lukewarm water, and rub gently with a soft cloth.

Makeshift ovens. When it is not practical to transport a factory-made reflector oven, a makeshift model can be patterned after the one created by Tom Baker on our Colorado hunt. The framework can be made from any type of sticks,

A makeshift reflector oven can be contrived from green sticks in little time. Here the author uses wire to assemble the basic framework. Note that the legs can be pressed into the earth to anchor the oven.

When the framework is completed, enclose the oven with the
heavy-duty aluminum foil pinched in place.

Anything can be baked in a reflector oven—meats, casseroles, and
even fish. But the most popular items are bread products and pastries, such as biscuits, cornbread, loaf bread, and sweetrolls.

as long as they are green. Wiring the frame together makes the oven more sturdy, but you can also lash it together with twine or even fishing line, if that's all you have. With either of these, however, cover the bindings with foil, or the exposure to intense heat for prolonged periods may weaken them. I use heavy-duty aluminum foil because of its durability. To hold it in place simply press, crimp, or pinch the foil as necessary around the framework of sticks. Be sure the shiny side of the foil is on the inside of the oven for maximum reflection.

Photos accompanying this chapter show the basic oven design to strive for, but don't worry about being exact in your measurements or having a finished oven that looks pretty. What's important is how it works. Two suggestions: First, assemble the frame so that the finished oven has short legs on the bottom. These can then be pushed gently into the ground when the oven is set before the fire, anchoring it securely even in strong breezes. Second, be sure the oven's baking shelf is sturdy; a pan of cake batter, or a pie or venison roast, can be relatively heavy. I usually reinforce the baking shelf with short cross-member sticks lashed in place.

"Quickies." The third type of reflector oven is a "quickie" effort that can be used in conjunction with any type of wire or mesh grill, or any type of heavy-duty grate installed in cooking areas designated by the U.S. Forest Service. In these cases, the actual reflector component of the "oven" is nothing more than a doubled-over sheet of heavy aluminum foil fashioned into a hood over the top of the enclosed baking area. Mold the hood by hand, attaching it to the grill by crimping the bottom edges of the foil around the cooking grate's outside frame. The nature of the stiff foil will keep the hood standing upright, and the front of the oven remains open so both the fire and food may be tended.

When using some type of wire grill, or the grate in a government campground, contrive a reflector hood from heavy foil. Here a ringneck pheasant slowly simmers to perfection.

Rocks

Biscuits

A nifty one-person reflector oven can be made by laying a new aluminum bread pan on its side, and setting biscuits or rolls on one of the pan's sidewalls.

Still another idea is to contrive a tiny one-person reflector oven from a new aluminum bread pan. This is perfect for the lone trail tramper who may occasionally like to prepare just enough biscuits or a small tray of cornbread to go with a bowl of stew. The bread pan should be set up so that it sits 2 inches off the ground on its side; the biscuits or other food sit on the shelf created by the side wall (see illustration). Also, it may be necessary halfway through the allotted baking time to move those food items at the front of the pan to the back, and those in back to the front.

HEATING THE OVEN

The best way to cook over fire is by letting the wood burn down to a bed of glowing, white-ash embers. And hardwood coals are best since they last longer than softwoods and won't impart undesirable flavors like conifers.

In reflector-oven cooking, different principles apply. Now, a high, open fire with plenty of flames is preferable, and this is more easily achieved and maintained with softwoods such as dry willow. Pine and similar resinous species can also be used since the flames and rising heat don't make direct contact with the food.

In reflector-oven cooking the heat of the fire is not used to cook the food directly in the customary sense. Instead, it cooks indirectly by having a continual quantity of radiant heat thrown onto the oven's angular, shiny walls. These, in turn, reflect it both upward and downward onto the baking shelf. In another manner of speaking, the baking process is almost the same as that in your oven at home, with two exceptions: The bright aluminum takes the place of the heating coils, but the aluminum itself is not the original source of the heat.

Boy Scouts use a solar cooker to roast their foil-wrapped hotdogs.

Since there is no temperature dial on a campfire, you'd best keep the fire well stoked. As necessary, regulate the baking temperature by adjusting the position of the oven in relation to its distance from the flames. If bread, biscuits, or other foods begin to brown just a little too quickly, move the oven away from the fire a bit. If flames temporarily die down a little, as when more fuel is being added, move it a little closer. For most types of reflector-oven cooking, you'll probably find yourself keeping the oven within 6 to 15 inches of the fire.

One additional tip has to do with the actual fire design. If you bank your fire at a slight angle, by propping up the far side of the kindling with small logs or rocks, the fire will have a tendency to throw more of its radiant heat toward the oven.

When using the hooded foil arrangement over a wire grill or U.S. Forest Service grate, the method varies slightly. Here, you'll want a small quantity of hardwood coals under

A reflector oven can even be used to supply a small camp with a modest amount of heat.

the food to cook it from the bottom, and a more robust fire directly in front of the hood for the aluminum to reflect onto the top of the food. However, arrangements such as this and others are ones that campers will have to engineer themselves, depending upon the dimensions of the grill or grate in question. Set foil-wrapped packages and baking meats directly on the grate. But for items such as biscuits, first cover the grill with a sheet of foil. Instead of making an enclosed hood over the top of the grill, you can also poke long sticks into the ground at an angle around the fire, then pinch sheets of aluminum foil in place over the sticks.

A reflector oven can even be used to supply a small camp with a modest amount of heat during cold weather. On frigid evenings or frosty mornings, you can "bounce" the warm glow of your campfire directly into a tent or lean-to, for example. With the flaps of the tent open, sleepers can enjoy as much as 10-degree temperature boost if the oven has been placed properly, is safe to operate during the night, and someone volunteers to stoke the fire occasionally. Two ovens placed side by side will make the inside of a tent or lean-to as much as 25 degrees warmer than the outside air temperature.

BAKING TECHNIQUES

The ideal way to bake or roast meats in a reflector oven is to wrap them in a foil pouch before setting them on the oven's baking shelf. I recommend meats no larger than three pounds — be it a single piece of beef or venison, or an aggregate quantity of individual chicken pieces or fish — wrapped with the bright side of the foil on the inside. The meat comes out exceptionally tender because the foil keeps the moisture from escaping, and the meat bastes slowly in its own juices. With meats that are rather dry or lean to begin with (certain fish species, game birds such as grouse and quail, and especially venison), add a bit of water to the bottom of the foil pouch or cover the meat with bacon strips or small dots of vegetable shortening.

It's also a good idea to about-face the foil meat packet about halfway through the required cooking time. When roasting gamebirds or other fowls, I turn back the top edges of the foil when the birds are almost finished to let them come to a crispy, golden brown on top.

A reflector oven does a yeoman's job of baking and roasting meats, but it does an even better job on bread products. It might seem like baking would be complicated in the backcountry, but it really isn't for those who plan in advance. Whether you intend to make bread, a pie, or whatever in camp, there are two efficient ways to go about it: The first is to begin at home by following your favorite recipe through its initial stages. Say, one night in camp your menu calls for a freeze dried ham and bean soup reconstituted with water, and you'd like to bake some cornbread to go with it. Before you leave, mix together at home all of the dry ingredients required for the cornbread recipe and secure them in a plastic bag. For ready identification, place a slip of paper inside the bag which describes the contents and working procedure.

The wet ingredients for most bread products or pastries seldom consist of more than a cup of water or milk, perhaps an egg, or a teaspoon or two of cooking oil or shortening. In the case of milk, you can use the powder form, packaged separately, then in camp reconstitute it with water. If transporting fresh eggs is out of the question, add dried egg powder at home, remembering to add water, over and above what the recipe calls for, to reconstitute the egg. Here is my cornbread recipe:

Camp Cornbread

1 cup yellow cornmeal
1 cup all-purpose white flour
2 tablespoons sugar
4 teaspoons baking powder
½ teaspoon salt
1 cup milk
¼ cup cooking oil or shortening
1 egg

At home, in a plastic bag add the cornmeal, flour, sugar, baking powder, and salt. In camp, mix in the milk, cooking oil, and egg until all ingredients are thoroughly blended. Pour the batter into a greased pan and set on the shelf in your reflector oven for ½ hour or until light brown on top. This recipe makes enough cornbread to serve three.

An even easier method: prepackaged mini-mixes from your local supermarket that state "add water only." Cakes, pie crusts, brownies, sweetrolls, biscuits, muffins – the list of such mixes commonly found in grocery stores is almost endless. They are quite inexpensive, too. As described in earlier chapters, you'll want to remove the contents from their cardboard boxes and repackage them in plastic bags. Many types of mixes come in paper envelopes which are easy to pack as is, but transfer them to plastic bags before you add the wet ingredients in camp. By thoroughly kneading the bag with your hands, you can mix the batter within the plastic pouch and eliminate having an extra pan or mixing bowl to clean.

As for which cornbread pan, cake pan, or pie tin to bake in, I often rely upon aluminum trays. When you buy convenience foods, save the trays they come in for later use on the trail. Or, in the houseware's department, you can buy

Baked goods are easy to make in camp with your reflector oven.
Buy premixed packages in your grocery store, then transfer the
contents to plastic bags with the cooking-instruction panel inside.

new aluminum, disposable trays of infinite sizes and shapes.
They weigh less than 1 ounce apiece and can easily be
stashed in your pack along with your other cooking gear.
The most versatile size, from my experience, measures 8
inches square by 2 inches high.

Other times I simply use heavy-duty aluminum foil to
make a pan. But it must be uniform in its dimensions for
your cornbread, cake, or other food to bake evenly. You
can press the foil around some other object to form a perfect shape; for instance, take a 14-inch square of heavy-
duty foil and press it around the bottom of a 9½-inch frying

For cornbread, muffins, pie crust, and other baked goods, you'll need some type of tray or pan. The author's daughter Lisa shows various sizes you can buy, and one she made by pressing foil around the bottom of a frypan.

pan, carefully remove it, fold over the upper edge to make a rim for added strength, and you have a tray for cornbread or cake batter. With a double thickness of heavy duty foil, you can make a pie tin.

For baking biscuits, sweetrolls, and similar breads in a reflector oven, again prepackage dry mixes at home. Then in camp add your wet ingredients and follow any other instructions for the particular recipe in question.

Baking Powder Biscuits

2 cups all-purpose white flour
3 teaspoons baking powder
1 teaspoon salt
¼ cup shortening or cooking oil
¾ cup milk

Place the flour, baking powder, and salt in a plastic bag. In camp, knead in the shortening or cooking oil, then begin slowly adding the milk until you have a soft, but not wet, dough. On a lightly floured surface continue to knead the dough about 25 times. Then press it out with your hands until it is about ½ inch thick. Cut out biscuits with your knife, then pop them into your reflector oven for 12 minutes, or until they are brown and done. To eliminate having to clean your oven afterward, set the biscuits on a sheet of clean foil instead of directly on the reflector's baking shelf. This recipe makes about 16 biscuits.

Most cookbook recipes for cakes, sweetrolls, cinnamon rolls, and other pastries are a bit lengthy and include some steps that are complicated to follow outdoors. This need not mean doing without cakes or other goodies—merely buy the prepackaged mini-mixes that only need water, and transfer them to plastic bags in the usual way. One happy exception to all of this is making a pie in camp, which anyone can tackle with the assurance of success. I usually use blackberries gathered along the way, but any other wild fruits or berries can be substituted in the following recipe; if weight is no problem, even canned berries or fruits work nicely.

Easy Pie Crust

2 cups sifted white flour
1 teaspoon salt
¾ cup shortening
¼ cup water

Mix flour and salt in a plastic bowl, then cut in the shortening thoroughly with a fork. Sprinkle in the water 1 tablespoon at a time until the flour is moistened but not too wet. Gather the dough into a ball, then divide it into two equal portions. On a lightly floured sheet of aluminum foil, roll out (or press with your hands) one of the balls of dough until it is about 2 inches larger in diameter than your 9-inch pie tin (made from a double thickness of heavy-duty foil). Then gently set the dough in the pan (the top edges of the dough should just barely overlap the rim of the pan). Next, add your pie filling (see recipe given here). Now roll out the second ball of dough, gently place it over the filling and with your fingertips crimp the edges together with the edges of the bottom layer of pie crust. Lightly sprinkle the top crust with sugar (optional), then make half a dozen 1-inch-long knife slits in the top crust to allow steam to escape. Bake approximately 45 minutes in your reflector oven before robust flames, turning the pie every 15 minutes until the crust is brown.

Blackberry Pie Filling

3 tablespoons flour
1 cup sugar
¼ teaspoon salt

4 cups fresh blackberries
2 tablespoons margarine

Mix the dry ingredients, then gently stir in the berries. Add the filling to the pie crust shell described above, then dot with pieces of margarine (or butter). In using canned berries, omit the salt, blend all of the ingredients, cook over a stove or fire until the juice thickens, then allow to cool before adding to the pie shell.

For bread in a reflector oven, I follow the sourdough recipe in Chapter 14. On your grocer's shelf you'll also find several varieties of "quick breads" that are entirely suitable for reflector-oven baking.

No matter what you cook, or whether your reflector oven is store-bought or makeshift, reflector-oven cooking is sure to add a new dimension to your outdoor dining.

13

The Versatile Dutch Oven

After traipsing around in the outdoors for a number of years, you are bound to acquire equipment preferences. You instinctively know from previous experiences what you need and what works out best for you. There is a particular knife, for instance, that always gets the nod while the others gather dust. There is a certain make of boot you consistently buy because it's more comfortable and sure-footed than the rest. You almost always don the same cherished hat.

So it is with cooking gear as well, and the types of meals you tend to rely on day in and day out. Cooking methods are equally individualistic, with one person sold on a gasoline backpack stove, another firmly believing his propane model is superior, and yet another, rain or shine, somehow managing a keyhole fire.

My fetish (after specific knives, boots, and hats) is a cast-iron dutch oven. It also is virtually foolproof for cooking and this makes it one of the most versatile pieces of equipment I've ever used. More than that, a dutch oven is durable, unbreakable, and, with the exception of routine cleaning, maintenance free. It also is quite inexpensive if prorated over a period of time. How many other items of outdoor gear do you own that cost less than $20 and will still be around long after you are gone? The dutch oven I have is already fifteen years old, has serviced hunting and fishing camps in at least twenty states, and is still in mint condition.

WHAT KIND TO BUY

I'm not exactly sure why, but in many parts of the country, particularly in small towns and other predominantly rural areas, dutch ovens are available in almost every store that carries hardware, housewares, sporting goods, or general merchandise.

Yet in metropolitan regions one can play hob just trying to explain to a salesperson what he wants. The problem is compounded by the fact that nowadays so many companies that manufacture cooking implements have at least one or two items in their line that they refer to as "dutch ovens" but really are poor imitations. A true dutch oven will have no components made of glass, plastic, or wood. And no true dutch oven will have a dome lid.

There also are many inexpensive copies of dutch ovens made of steel, pig iron, and aluminum. Forget them. The pig iron and steel models will rust. And none of the three is capable of efficiently taking and evenly distributing heat in and throughout their cooking surfaces. What happens, then, is that hot spots develop, causing food to burn and stick. After only a year or two of use, the steel and aluminum models warp, so that their lids no longer fit properly.

Every outdoorsman has equipment preferences, but a cast-iron dutch oven is one item that does it all. Use it for frying, baking, boiling, or slow-simmering any type of food imaginable.

What you want is an original cast-iron dutch oven. It may have a capacity of 2, 4, 6, or 8 quarts (I recommend either the 4- or 6-quart models for trail use), and carry one of many different brand names, but the design is traditionally very well defined.

First, the pot has a flat bottom, slightly sloping sides, and stands on three short legs. It also has a very strong wire bail. The lid fits fairly tightly, and it has an integrated cast-iron handle in the middle. Further, the lid has a slightly convex shape, but with an upright rim or flange around its diameter to hold coals. Any deviation from this basic, time-tested design may rightly be something for cooking, but it's not a real dutch oven and won't perform as many culinary feats.

Don't settle for a cheap imitation. Look for an original cast-iron dutch oven like the one shown here. Note the flange around the lid for holding coals, the wire bail, and the three legs.

If cast-iron dutch ovens are not readily available in your region, I can suggest four sources: My oven, a very good one, was made by the Lodge Manufacturing Company, South Pittsburg, Tennessee 37380, but I recommend as well those sold by L.L. Bean, Freeport, Maine 04033, Herter's Inc., Mitchell, South Dakota 57301, and General Housewares Corporation, P.O. Box 4066, Terre Haute, Indiana 47804.

To be sure, a cast-iron dutch oven is on the heavy side (my 6-quart model weighs 15 pounds) and therefore is not suited for use by strict, ultralight backpackers. But for some outings, a dutch oven may be justified. Say, there are four members in the party, you'll be away only for a weekend, and your food requirements are minimal — you can shoulder or share the extra weight.

Perhaps other circumstances prevail. It's midsummer, the weather is as clear as a bell, so you decide to leave your tent at home and sleep under the stars. Without that extra 8 pounds, maybe you can take a small dutch oven. Or you might be traveling by canoe, four-wheel drive, or on horseback through rugged terrain to set up a base camp in the boonies, and from there each day striking out on foot to explore the nearby territory; likely, the base camp can benefit from the presence of a dutch oven. Maybe an outfitter has already gone into the backcountry with a packtrain and set up a base camp for you and your pals (this increasingly popular concept is called "drop-camping"), and all you have to do is hike in later with your personal stuff, like clothes and fishing tackle; each of your packs therefore weighs only 8 or 10 pounds, so you have a chance to do some dutch-oven cooking.

It's worth noting that the hefty weight of a dutch oven is its major advantage. Many cooking efforts on the trail or in camp are accomplished over coals with no dials to control accurately the heat your food is subjected to. Even with

Before using a dutch oven for the first time, "season" the cast iron by impregnating its porous surface with cooking oil and then "baking" it in an oven. Also, swab all inner surfaces with oil if the dutch oven is not to be used for a while.

high-quality gasoline and propane stoves, temperatures may be highly irregular over the course of prolonged cooking periods. But a cast-iron dutch oven takes heat more slowly, distributes it more evenly, holds it longer, and thereby allows for failsafe cooking. In short, it is difficult to make a mistake with a dutch oven because the personality of cast iron makes up for almost any error on the part of the cook.

The first order of business with a new dutch oven is to clean it. Submerge both pot and lid in hot, soapy water and thoroughly scrub them down with a stiff bristle brush. This removes the Cosmoline preservative the manufacturer has applied to the surface of the porous metal. Now, rinse the oven well and towel dry it.

Next it is necessary to "season" the metal. The easiest way is by smearing the inside of the pot and the underneath side of the lid liberally with cooking oil (some use lard, rendered beef suet, or bacon fat, but these can smoke up your kitchen). Then place the pot and the lid in your oven at 350° and let them "bake" for an hour. Use a basting brush every fifteen minutes to wipe the inside metal surfaces with more oil.

After this initial seasoning, little additional maintenance is ever needed. To clean the oven after a meal, you seldom need to do more than wipe out the inside surfaces with paper towels or a damp cloth. Food deposits and juices should come away easily because of the Teflon-like surface the cast iron achieved through the seasoning process. After wiping the inside, wash the inside of the oven with just a touch of mild detergent and completely rinse with scalding-hot water to kill germs. Finally, towel dry the oven or let it drip dry. Absolutely never let any type of cast-iron implement soak for a long time in dishwater, and don't use steel-wool scouring pads; both will ruin the seasoning on the metal's surfaces. Lastly, any time your dutch oven is to go more than a few days before being used, don't put it away until you have lightly swabbed its inside surfaces with a paper towel and a tablespoon or two of cooking oil or lard.

FRYING FOODS ON THE LID

When it's my turn to cook, I'll usually climb out of the sack a little earlier than usual so I can prepare both breakfast and supper simultaneously. I begin by building a robust fire that will have become a bed of glowing coals by the end of breakfast. Hardwoods work best for this because the embers last much longer than those from softwoods.

When the fire produces its first coals, I rake some away

By turning the dutch-oven lid upside down and setting it directly on coals you can fry foods such as bacon and eggs.

Foods fried in a dutch-oven lid never taste greasy because the grease drains to the center of the concave lid, where it can easily be spooned away.

for the breakfast cooking. As I said before, dutch ovens are very versatile, so much so that I often don't even take a frying pan along. I simply use the lid of may dutch oven to fry bacon, eggs, potatoes, or somedays even flapjacks or french toast — no need to bring along a frying pan. Simply turn the lid upside-down and put it directly on the coals.

You can fry hamburgers this way, too, as well as sausage, small steaks, chops, fresh fish, or almost anything else you choose. There is even a distinct advantage to frying on a slightly concave surface like this. A common complaint about fried foods is that they taste too greasy and don't always set well with one's internal plumbing. But with an inverted dutch-oven-lid frypan, foods never taste greasy if, after the food is about one-third cooked, you begin pushing it away from the center so that it surrounds the lid's outer perimeter. Oils, greases, and drippings collect in a small puddle in the middle of the concave surface of the lid; just spoon them off as they accumulate.

BELOW-GROUND SLOW ROASTING

Before we got sidetracked, we were engaged in the morning cooking. As my partners are eating their breakfast, I set to the task of preparing the evening meal. The first step is to place the dutch oven close to the coals so that it will begin to absorb heat. Meanwhile, I peel vegetables, potatoes, and get out whatever other ingredients or spices may be needed.

Then with a shovel or entrenching tool, I dig a hole about 1½ feet deep and 15 inches in diameter. It takes only a few minutes. Next, I usually place a large (3 or 4 pound) beef or venison roast in the dutch-oven pot, along with several tablespoons of oil, set the oven on the coals and sear the meat on all sides until it is lightly browned. Then I fill the remainder of the dutch oven (on top of the meat and around it) with sliced potatoes, onions, carrots, green peppers, celery, or whatever other vegetables are in camp. Finally, I add 2 cups of water, sprinkle on a little salt and pepper, and put on the lid.

Now, take one-third of your glowing, red coals and shovel them into the bottom of the hole you've dug. Set your dutch-oven dinner into the hole on top of the coals, then shovel on top of the oven the remaining two-thirds of the coals on top of it. After that, loosely shovel an inch of dirt for insulation on top (no more, or you'll smother the coals).

The hot embers packed around the dutch oven will allow your supper to bubble and simmer very slowly to perfection while you and your cohorts are out chasing fish or game during the day. Don't give your meal another thought. Nothing will burn. Nothing will dry out. Nothing will get cold. The pot roast and fixin's will be cooked and ready to eat in about three hours. But if the evening fishing is too good to pass up, or it takes more time than you figured to haul out your deer, the food will remain tender, juicy, piping hot, and delicious for twelve hours or more, depending upon the type and amount of coals.

To retrieve your dinner, carefully scrape away the thin layer of dirt covering the dutch oven. Then use a glove or a handmade coat-hanger tool to reach down into the pit and lift the oven out by its wire bail. In the bottom of the dutch oven will have collected an ample quantity of hot juices and broth that can be ladled over the meat, potatoes, and vegetables. Or the liquid can be thickened into a superb, rich gravy by stirring in a few teaspoons of flour.

I'll testify that not many things are more satisfying than climbing the last steep hill back to camp at day's end, sliding out of heavy boots and into moccasins, perhaps having a

Below-ground roasting with a dutch oven produces excellent meals. Here, after searing a venison pot roast on all sides, the author first adds carrots, potatoes, and other vegetables. Use freeze-dried or dehydrated vegetables if you choose.

Next, shovel one-third of your coals into a pit, lower the dutch oven into the hole, and set it on top of the embers.

Shovel the remaining two-thirds of the coals on top of the oven's lid.

With coals on top of and around the sides of the dutch oven, your meal will bubble slowly to perfection. Shovel on one inch of dirt on top of the coals to insulate the oven.

slug of Old Stumpblower, and relishing the thought that supper already is cooked, hot, and waiting.

Below-ground roasting doesn't have to be restricted to standard meat-and-potatoes meals using beef or venison roasts, however. Why not try a pork roast with sauerkraut? Or chicken pieces, gamebirds, large chunks of freshly caught fish made into a thick soup, or ham and beans?

A handy tool for lifting the dutch oven from the pit by its wire bail is easily fashioned from coat-hanger wire.

ABOVE-GROUND SIMMERING AND BAKING

Trail cooks can also use dutch ovens to create hearty chowders, soups, stews, bean dishes, chili, or other favorite one-pot meals above ground. If someone in the party will be in or around camp all day, just instruct him to keep the fire merrily flickering away, with the oven sitting nearby. Just turn the oven occasionally and be sure a small quantity of coals is always on top of the lid. Whenever you straggle in, you simply dish out your meal.

Of course, there may be times when several buddies can rationalize having a dutch oven in camp, but find it impossible to bring along fresh vegetables and meats. As substitutes, use canned meats and vegetables. Or, better yet, use freeze-dried vegetables, dehydrated soup mixes, dried meats, jerky, or other lightweight, nonperishable foods. All will swell up into tender morsels after an hour or two in the bubbling cauldron.

I'd like to pass along my unbeatable chili recipe (every chili nut feels the same way about his own particular concoction). The ingredients are admittedly heavy, but if you were able to take a dutch oven in the first place, they don't constitute all that much more weight.

John's Chili

2 pounds deerburger or
  hamburger
1 green pepper, diced
2 15-ounce cans red kidney
  beans
2 15-ounce cans tomato sauce
1 tablespoon cayenne pepper
1 tablespoon garlic powder

1 large clove minced
  garlic
1 teaspoon cumin seed
1 teaspoon salt
2 bay leaves, broken
1 tablespoon dried onion
  flakes
4 tablespoons chili powder

The dry ingredients can be premixed at home and placed in a plastic bag. In camp, brown the deerburger or hamburger until it is done, then spoon away any grease that has collected. Add all the other ingredients, bring to a boil, quickly reduce the heat and then slowly simmer for 2 hours. You may want to add water to make the dish a bit more soupy, depending on the amount of water packed with the beans of the particular brand you buy. The recipe serves six.

Above-ground baking in a dutch oven is fast and efficient. Lay biscuits in the bottom of the oven, for instance, and set the oven on top of a small quantity of coals with a heaping shovelful on top of the lid.

Biscuits take only a few minutes to bake, so don't go far away. Use your coat-hanger tool to lift lid and check their progress, to be sure they don't burn.

Above-ground baking in a dutch oven is easy, too. Biscuits are a ready example. As with reflector-oven cooking, mix your dry ingredients at home and plastic bag 'em along with a slip of paper inside describing wet ingredients to be added in camp. Use the baking-powder-biscuit recipe in Chapter 12 or the sourdough-biscuit mix in Chapter 14 if you do not already have a favorite recipe of your own.

Later, roll out your dough, cut the biscuits to size, allow them to rise a bit while wiping the bottom of the dutch oven with oil, then lay the biscuits in place so they are barely touching. Put on the lid, then set the dutch oven on top of just a very small number of coals. Finally, heap a shovelful of coals on top of the lid. But don't go away; lift the lid every two minutes to check the biscuits—they will bake very quickly. You can bake bread in camp the same way (I like the sourdough recipe given in Chapter 14) by molding the loaf by hand, letting it rise, then laying it in the bottom of the oven. However, use slightly less coals on the lid: the thicker dough will require a longer baking time, and you don't want the top crust to burn.

Bake cornbread or a cake in a dutch oven, as well. Prepare your dry mix at home in the usual manner (or use a prepackaged mix), in camp add water to make a batter, pour it into a small aluminum foil tray, and set the works in the bottom of the oven with coals again on top of the lid. Or make a pie from wild berries gathered around camp, following the pie crust mix and filling recipe given in Chapter 12 and then setting the pie pan in the bottom of the dutch oven.

Two tips First, if there is any possible way to have two dutch ovens along, one a bit smaller than the other, you can use them simultaneously, with a technique called "stack baking." The utility of this idea primarily has to do with conserving firewood and coals.

Simply establish a good bed of coals and rake a small quantity aside. Place the first, larger oven on top of the coals, then put coals on the lid. Now, stack the second oven right on top of the first so the coals on top of the lid of the

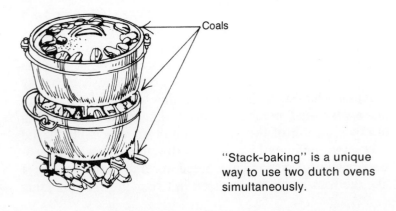

Coals

"Stack-baking" is a unique way to use two dutch ovens simultaneously.

A small whiskbroom is handy in camp for sweeping soot and ashes from the lid of the dutch oven before serving the fare inside.

first oven heat the underneath side of the second oven. Finally, place another quantity of coals on the lid of the top oven.

Second, since much of a dutch oven's use has to do with piling quantities of embers on top of the lid, a handy item to have on hand is a small whiskbroom. Among its countless uses around camp, it is perfect for sweeping soot and ashes off the oven's lid before it is removed and the meal set before your eager companions. If you don't have a whiskbroom, a thick, elongated swatch of green grass works nearly as well; be careful not to burn your fingers, though.

My old, reliable cast-iron dutch oven—it's a tad too heavy for every trail-cooking adventure, but when it's along it's worth its weight in good eating.

14

Sourdough Cooking

It was agreed upon. We'd rise by 5 a.m. and be on the water plugging for pike by 6. Normally it would take several good pokes with a cattle prod to roust me at such an ungodly hour, but this time turned out to be different. Shortly after 4 a.m. the fragrant, tantalizing aromas of fresh sourdough bread and hot coffee wafted through the flaps of our mountain tent and immediately brought me to my feet. Seconds later I was hobbling across frosty Canadian pebblestone to the fire where Stuart Gess was busily preparing baked goods for our camp kitchen.

Following our customary procedure, our fishing party of six had launched upon the first leg of our annual search for pike in the Limestone River country of northern Manitoba. And Gess, who cares more about outdoor cooking than fishing, had once again repeated his ritual of staying up the first night and building a supply of the most delicious sourdough goodies I've ever sunk my teeth into.

Rumor has it Gess hasn't eaten store-bought bread in nearly thirty years, at home or on the trail, and I believe it. Around the fire he'd set up four reflector ovens that now contained the beginnings of delectable breads, biscuits, and muffins. And in a dutch oven near the coals I peeped a look at a sourdough cake that was just starting to rise.

Stu quickly sliced me a couple of inch-thick slabs from a warm loaf of bread, which I slathered with wild honey and devoured before he could even stir the coals. Then with a turnkey I opened a tin of butter and liberally coated two more slices. This hearty repast I washed down with a cup of coffee just the way I like it — coal black and almost thick enough to plow.

Moments later three more hungry anglers, including our Cree guide Jimmy Bartok, were huddled around the make-shift bakery, eager to get in on the action. Nobody seemed to notice or care about bare feet on almost frozen ground. When two more sleepy-eyed members climbed out of their eiderdown bags with their noses twitching an hour before the formal breakfast call, Gess expressed his indignation in a dramatic tirade. But, then, as he had done many times before, he grinned, picked up the spatula he'd disgustedly thrown to the ground upon witnessing his kitchen being ransacked, and set about preparing our breakfast.

I can't recall how the fishing was that day, but indelibly imprinted in my mind are fond remembrances of the meal placed before us. Sourdough pancakes drooled with Vermont maple syrup. Side orders of eggs, crisp walleye fillets, and hashbrowns soon followed. And, if this weren't enough, Stu then placed in front of our bulging eyes, and stomachs, a batch of muffins to mop our plates. These contained raisins and chopped walnuts, and were covered with icing.

While the rest of us began breaking camp, Gess made sandwiches for our lunch bags, from sourdough bread, of course, with fillings of assorted cheeses and cold meats. There would be generous chunks of chocolate cake to nibble on, too.

With that, we pushed off in our canoes. Our strategy on this trip was no big secret, because we've been doing it the same way for many years. We casually fish our way downstream, following the Limestone to its confluence with Dog Lake, where a floatplane shuttles us back to civilization. At select spots along the way pointed out by our Indian friend, we beach our boats, shoulder lightweight packs, grab a couple of rods, and hike the mile or two inland to nearby lakes. We eat lunch while we fish on foot around the shoreline. Supper is later cooked on two backpack stoves or a wood fire somewhere along the lakefront. About an hour before dusk we hike back to our canoes tied up at the riverbank and pitch a modest tent camp for still another one-night stand. The whole episode repeats itself the next day. By the end of the week our beards are beginning to scratch, muscles we had forgotten we had now feel like they're tied in knots, the mosquitoes have unmercifully chewed us to tatters, and we're just possibly the happiest men in the world.

"STARTER"

Sourdough is wonderfully suited to almost any type of outing. Contrary to popular legend, it does not have its origin in the era of the historical gold strikes in Alaska and the Yukon, nor even earlier when settlers were pioneering new territories beyond the Mississippi. Credit must be given to the Marquis de Rochambeau, who in 1725 brought sourdough from France to Rhode Island. Later, it was a staple of French and Revolutionary Army troops in their joint effort against the British.

Only after that did early homesteaders realize its usefulness and begin to carry it with them as they explored the new frontier. It was actually 100 years later, during the gold rush of the Northwest, that sourdough began to enjoy great popularity with grizzled prospectors who themselves were sometimes referred to as "sourdoughs" because of their cantankerous personalities. (Accidentally spilled sourdough batter will annoyingly stick like cement to anything it touches and has even been known to corrode metal surfaces.)

For those people living in rugged wilderness country, bread products were a vital necessity, but it might be weeks (or months) until the next supply train or trader would be traveling through with needed provisions. To have a continual bread supply on hand, sourdough "starter" was a lifesaver because it constantly "renewed" itself, from a small portion of the original. Consequently, a river steamer loaded with supplies could find itself delayed by winter ice, or a trader mushing his dogsled through deep winter snow could be very late in making his rounds, yet a prospector, trapper, or dirt farmer living in the backcountry could nevertheless continue to put bread on the table.

Sourdough, then, was not really "invented" out of a desire for delicious baked goods but as a means toward self-sufficiency. Yet it was a happy coincidence that sourdough turned out to be lip-smacking good, and gradually it worked its way from the outback to some of the most famous dining establishments in this country. To this day, exclusive restaurants from Juneau to as far south as San Francisco bake sourdough breads and biscuits claimed to be derived from yeast starters still in existence that were begun as early as 1850.

All sourdough cooking, then, begins with starter, which not only serves as the base for today's baking but ensures tomorrow's as well. On the trail it can be made from scratch one day, then used for cooking each day thereafter. But for convenience, and since starter can be kept indefinitely, I keep a supply at home in my refrigerator and then simply take some with me.

To prepare starter you'll need three basic ingredients: yeast, flour, and water. In a plastic or glass bowl mix two ¼-ounce packets of dry yeast in 2 cups of warm water (105°–115°) and then add 2 cups of flour. Mix well to produce a syrupy batter, which should be covered with a towel or loose-fitting lid and placed in a warm spot overnight. In the morning you'll have a bubbly, frothy starter (called a "sponge" by die-hard sourdough experts) that smells clean, sour, and almost alcoholic.

Each time you're ready to bake you'll need approximately 2 cups of starter. To ensure a continual supply, the night before you plan to bake add 2 cups of water and 2 cups of flour to the existing starter, stir well and place in a warm spot. The next morning you'll have a double batch of starter, half of which is used for the baking and the other half retained to perpetuate the cycle.

But before cooking, let's backtrack just a bit to mention a few crucial elements in the mixing, storage, and use of your starter.

- Sourdough starter contains acid that will react with any metal it contacts and in so doing will assume a "tinny" flavor. Always use mixing bowls and utensils made of glass, plastic or wood.

- Never add anything else to the starter you're saving except additional flour and water when you want to increase the supply, or you may kill the bacterial yeast organisms and curtail the fermentation process that keeps the starter alive and yields its unique flavor. By the same token, cold starter taken right from your refrigerator is alive but inactive and should not be used in this state. Allow it to sit out overnight in a warm place before preparing your recipe. (On the trail, when it's very cold, place your starter in the bottom of your sleeping bag overnight to increase its temperature.)

- For storing starter, I keep mine in the refrigerator in a large glass jar with a loose-fitting screw-cap lid that allows gases to escape. If the starter remains in the refrigerator for several months without being activated for cooking purposes, you'll begin to notice the formation of a clear or amber-colored liquid floating on the surface. This is normal, so pay it no mind, but do thoroughly stir it into the starter prior to its next use.

For trail use, I like to transfer about 2 cups of starter from my refrigerator glass jar to a small prechilled ironstone crock that has a loose-fitting lid, wire bail, and rubber gasket. You can find pewter crocks containing various cheese spreads in the dairy section of your grocery store.

These containers are sturdy but a mite on the heavy side. And you have to remember to keep the starter cool, or it will begin to expand—thus the prechilled crock, loose-fitting lid, and recommendation the starter vessel be placed in a cold stream overnight when camping in warm weather.

For those who travel extremely light and can't be inconvenienced with moist starter in a crockery vessel or the need to maintain it at a cool temperature, a good alternative is dried starter. Simply spoon gobs of starter from your jar at home onto the shiny side of a sheet of waxed paper and cover with another sheet. Then press the individual gobs of starter into round cookie-like shapes about 2 inches in di-

The easiest way to store starter at home is in a plastic pitcher in your refrigerator. Note removable lid with a vent cap slightly ajar to allow gases to escape.

One way to transport two cups of starter for outdoor baking is in a pewter crock like this one. Cheese spreads come in these containers, which are available in most grocery stores.

When traveling light, spoon gobs of sourdough starter onto waxed paper and let it dry. Store in plastic bags. In camp, reconstitute by letting the starter "cookies" soak in warm water.

ameter. Let these "cookies" dry completely, turning every few hours to speed the process, and then stow them in a plastic bag. When you need 2 cups of starter in camp, thoroughly crumbld 6 of the starter cookies in a plastic bowl until they are powdery, then stir in 2 cups of warm water and let the works sit in a warm spot overnight.

Several commercially available dry sourdough starter mixes are also on the market. They come in paper packets and usually can be found in food specialty shops or the mail-order catalogs of companies that sell camping foods. All that's necessary to reconstitute these dry mixes into starter is the addition of warm water. I find these mixes do not quite measure up to the quality of homemade starter, but for ultralight trail cooking they are more than acceptable.

PANCAKES, BISCUITS, AND OTHER DELIGHTS

Sourdough pancakes are remarkably easy to prepare, and they are the lightest I've ever tasted. Yet they will easily fortify you for the morning's hiking, hunting, or fishing. When making them in the company of others, just watch out for the stampede!

Sourdough Pancakes

2 cups starter
1 egg (fresh or reconstituted
 equivalent)
2 tablespoons sugar

4 tablespoons cooking oil
1 teaspoon baking soda
4 tablespoons water

Mix the starter, egg, sugar, and oil in a plastic bowl so it is thoroughly blended. In a separate cup dissolve the soda in the water and then gently fold it into the pancake batter. Then spoon the pancake batter into a liberally greased frypan in the usual way, or use the inverted lid of a dutch oven. This recipe serves three hungry campers. For variety, you might add a handful of chopped nuts to the batter, fresh wild blackberries you have gathered, or freeze-dried banana chips from your trail snack pouch (let any dried fruits or berries soak in a pan of water for 15 minutes to swell up slightly before adding them to the pancake batter).

Sourdough Muffins

2 cups starter
1 teaspoon salt
1 egg (fresh or dehydrated equivalent)
¼ cup cooking oil
¼ cup milk (dry-milk powder with water added later)
1½ cups all-purpose white flour
¼ cup sugar
3 teaspoons baking powder

Of the many sourdough concoctions, pancakes are a universal favorite. For variety, add dried banana chips or fresh blackberries or blueberries.

Mix the "wet" ingredients together, then stir in the "dry" ingredients until the flour is just barely moistened. If the mix seems too thick and dry, add a bit more water. If it's too soupy, add just a little more flour. Meanwhile, someone should prepare a number of muffin "tins": press individual 6-inch squares of heavy-duty aluminum foil around the bottom of a drinking cup or coffee cup. Fill them ³/₄ full and set them in your reflector oven until the muffins are golden brown on top. You can also use a dutch oven, by placing coals on the lid. The above recipe makes 12 muffins but can be varied in countless ways. Substitute whole-wheat flour for the white, or use an equal mixture of both. Add finely chopped nuts to the batter, fresh wild blueberries, or any dried fruits that have first been reconstituted with water.

Sourdough Biscuits

2 cups starter
3/4 teaspoon baking soda
2 eggs (fresh or powdered equivalent)
2 tablespoons cooking oil
Enough flour to make a stiff dough

Gently mix all ingredients. If you have used powdered eggs, add the required water. The dough should be stiff and moist, but not sticky. Lay out a sheet of aluminum foil and sprinkle a bit of flour on top of it. Then roll out the dough or pat it with your hands so it is about ½ inch thick. Cut out biscuit-size shapes with your knife. (The biscuits will be lighter and fluffier if you cover them with a cloth and let them rise for an hour before baking.) Place the biscuits on a sheet of lightly greased foil in your reflector oven or in the bottom of your dutch oven. These biscuits can even be baked in a frying pan on an open fire. Lightly grease the bottom of the skillet and put it on your cooking grill until the bottoms of the biscuits just barely begin to turn brown. Then remove the pan from the fire and prop it up at a sharp angle next to the flames to allow the tops to brown, turning the pan occasionally so all the biscuits are exposed to adequate heat. This recipe makes one dozen hefty biscuits; any leftovers can be nibbled on the trail.

Sourdough Bread

2 cups starter
1 envelope dry yeast (¼ ounce size)
2 teaspoons sugar
2 teaspoons salt
1 teaspoon baking soda
5 cups flour
1½ cups very warm water

Hundreds of years ago homesteaders did not add additional yeast to their sourdough bread, other than what was already in the starter. But for a much lighter bread, most modern cooks prefer to do so. Dissolve the yeast in the warm water and add it to the starter. Then stir in the sugar, salt, and 3 cups of flour. Beat the mixture vigorously for

Sourdough biscuits are sure to find favor with active outdoorsmen. These are being baked in a reflector oven.

several minutes with a wooden spoon and then cover the bowl with a towel and let it sit in a warm place until the dough doubles in volume (about one and a half hours). Mix the baking soda with one cup of the remaining flour and knead it into the dough. Transfer the dough to a sheet of aluminum foil that has been lightly floured and knead it until it is smooth and elastic (5 to 10 minutes), adding flour as necessary to keep the dough from sticking. Depending upon the size of your baking equipment, shape the dough into a large round loaf or two small ones, cover with a towel, and let rise again in a warm place for another hour, or until it has doubled in size. Now bake in your reflector oven on a sheet of greased aluminum foil or in the bottom of a greased dutch oven until the crust is brown and the loaf gives a hollow sound when you tap it with your fingers.

Regarding all the recipes given here, it's wise to try them at home first to make sure you have them down pat. In some cases, quantities of certain ingredients may have to be slightly adjusted.

If you are camping and cooking at higher altitudes, use a bit more baking soda or baking powder to help bread or biscuit dough rise more. Also, flour readily absorbs moisture from the air, so if you happen upon damp or very humid weather, any recipe may require slightly more flour than called for; conversely, in arid climates slightly less flour (or slightly more water) may result in the best mix.

Sourdough starter also can simply be added to many prepackaged mini-mixes (those for cakes or muffins, for instance). Just add one cup of starter, then follow the directions that come with the mix.

Finally, as described in Chapter 2, many recipes can be simplified by premixing dry ingredients (flour, sugar, salt and so on) at home and securing them in labeled plastic bags. In camp, then, all that's necessary is the addition of your starter and other wet ingredients.

15

Ultralight Trail Cooking

"I don't care if it's a world-record-class animal," John Barnes griped. "Don't ever again let me shoot another moose this far in the backcountry. If you have to, take my rifle away from me, or shout and wave your arms and scare the moose away before I have a chance to pull the trigger."

We were somewhere in Ontario's bush, and my partner and I were so exhausted we were ready to drop. We had hiked far into the hinterland with full packs, sleeping bags, a two-man tent, rifles, and enough provisions for a week. And the task we now faced was carrying 600 pounds of moose meat, plus the hide and horns, through eight miles of boggy sprucelands and jumbled Canadian shield granite.

Looking back, it probably was the most physically taxing work I have ever done at any time in my life, or ever hope to do again. One thing we did gain, however, in addition to a full appreciation for how big a moose really was, was a first-hand education in the art of lightweight trail cooking. No, make that *ultra*light cooking.

When the big moose was down, the first order of business was to skin it out, rough-quarter the meat, stow most of the venison in cloth game bags suspended high out of the reach of bears, and with 25 pounds of meat apiece (in addition to our other gear) hike back to our truck parked at the trailhead. There we shed as much weight as possible so that each subsequent journey back into the bush would allow us to pack out as much meat as we could carry, to reduce the overall number of trips we'd have to make.

"We won't need our rifles, ammo, binoculars or any of that stuff," John suggested. "And since the weather is clear we can do without our tent and sleep under the stars. For each trip we have to make, let's take just our sleeping bags, packframes, rope, and enough food for three meals, one during the hike in, one at the moose-kill site at night, and one coming out. If we limit our packs to no more than 6 pounds apiece we should be able to each carry out 75 pounds of meat per trip. On the final trek we'll bring out the cape and antlers."

Getting our packs down to the 6-pound maximum required a good deal of planning and, if anything, our chosen food and cooking equipment played a crucial role because the sleeping bags alone weighed 2 pounds each. Add another 2 pounds apiece for our aluminum packframes. The lashing rope which I carried tipped the balance at $\frac{1}{2}$ pound, as did a small whetstone and bone-cutting saw that Barnes carried. That left us each an allowance of only $1\frac{1}{2}$ pounds for cooking and eating gear and food!

We each had our one-person mess kits and in the utensil department took only one spoon apiece (resorting to our sheath knives for any cutting chores that might be necessary). Instead of toting the prohibitive weight of even a lightweight trail stove and fuel bottle, we cooked our meals over spartan fires. Streams, small lakes, and beaver ponds speckled the countryside so there was no need for canteens.

To ensure water purity we each had a ½-ounce Super Straw Water Filter (see Chapter 7) for use during intermittant sips from our Sierra cups. (When water was needed for cooking we boiled it.) The meals over the five-day period consisted of assorted high-carbohydrate backpack rations such as freeze-dried casseroles, flavored noodle mixes, powdered eggs, dehydrated potatoes and vegetables, rice, beef and chicken bouillon cubes, powdered fruit juices, and instant puddings. Not glamorous food, to be sure, except on the two occasions we savored broiled moose tenderloin, but it was more than adequate for our nutritional needs and tasty, too.

There are other occasions, as well, when 'packers need to travel extremely light. One woman I know, for example, is an amateur geologist and rock hound who every year spends several weeks exploring the famous mining regions near Lynn Lake, Manitoba. She seldom returns to the trailhead without a knapsack full of uranium samples, copper, nickle, mica, and quartz. Hefting that kind of payload would be impossible if she didn't travel with lightweight equipment, and food and cooking gear are two places where she pares her provisions to the bone.

I also take the ultralight trail-cooking route when I'm doing wildlife photography on magazine assignments because camera equipment is incredibly heavy. I've never actually weighed the gear that usually accompanies me, but I'll testify that two cameras, two lenses, other attachments, a tripod, and as many as 100 rolls of color film are so burdensome, I absolutely have to trim every possible ounce.

Even when it's not mandatory, ultralight trail cooking is sometimes just plain fun; many outdoor cooks enjoy testing their skills in the preparation of new and exciting menus with the meagerest assortment of gear conceivable. Liken it, if you will, to the angler who knows he can catch trout on

Many backpackers are go-light purists who find great satisfaction in paring every ounce to the bone.

a hook baited with a big gob of nightcrawlers but derives far greater satisfaction from the challenge of using dry flies or nymphs.

Whether to use a trail stove or prepare meals over an open fire is something you have to decide for yourself. I use both methods because I like to be versatile.

OPEN-FIRE COOKING

On those particular adventures in which every ounce counts, open-fire cooking is most likely to get the nod. Here, you need few essentials other than waterproof matches. Any of the fire designs described in Chapter 8 will suffice if they are accordingly scaled down to accommodate the reduced sizes of the cooking gear that necessarily will be coming into play.

An ideal grill for this type of cooking is the hollow aluminum, rectangular affair that weighs only 4 ounces and is commonly found in backpacking and camping supply stores. I know some devout 'packers who look upon even this as excessively heavy, however, and in its place substitute a simple length of coathanger wire bent into a tight S-curve; it amply supports a tiny pot or frypan and tips the scales at a gossamer ½ ounce.

Relying on matches alone for establishing a cooking fire is risky because you might encounter rain, snow, or sleet

Hollow-tube, aluminum backpacking grill is favored by many ultralight packers. It measures 4 by 14 inches and weighs 4½ oz.

and have difficulty finding dry wood. To hedge their bets a little, and guarantee easy fire starting even with damp wood, many trail trampers make room in their duffle for a Metal Match or Magnesium Fire Starter. They also have along a 1-ounce container or homemade tinder.

I use two types of tinder on a regular basis. During anticipated mild weather conditions the tinder I rely upon most frequently, and admittedly have never seen recommended elsewhere, is a 35mm plastic film canister (with a snap-top lid to ensure the contents remain dry) filled with, of all things, dryer lint. Every home clothes dryer these days, whether gas or electric, has an easily removable lint screen that at least once a week becomes clogged with all kinds of tiny threads and fabric fluff. This lint is highly flammable, yet it is very much like the goosedown found in jackets and sleeping bags in that a large quantity can easily be compressed into only a fraction of its original size. You can literally stuff a big handful of this lint into a film can. Then, merely take out a little pinch when needed, fluff it up to golf ball size and touch a match to it.

When I'm anticipating inclement weather and the use of dry tinder alone may result in exasperating fire-building difficulties, I fill a film can with Mautz Fire Ribbon Paste from my larger squeeze tube at home. This incredible stuff, described in Chapter 8, will burn on water, snow, or ice, and causes even sopping wet wood to ignite eventually.

My friend Al Wolter, who works for the U.S. Forest Service in Duluth, Minnesota, and thereby is privileged to spend more time outdoors than any one person deserves, takes a somewhat different tack. He fills a 35mm film canister with several small pieces of Celotex that have been soaked in kerosene. Celotex is a very porous fiberboard material commonly used as a sheathing to cover the stud-framing of a house before the exterior siding is nailed in place. Visit a site where a new home is being built and you'll find scraps of the stuff lying around. A piece ¾ inch thick by 2 feet square should last you many years.

A failsafe fire-starting aid you can make at home is a scrap of Celotex fireboard material soaked in kerosene and stored in a 35mm film can.

However, I'll offer one special word of precaution: Soak your small pieces of Celotex in kerosene only. Kerosene has a very low flash point, which means it ignites easily but safely and burns slowly with a relatively hot flame. Never use a high flash-point fuel such as gasoline, which is so volatile it literally explodes when ignited. If damp wood occasionally is a problem, a single kerosene-soaked Celotex cube placed beneath a small stack of pencil-size sticks will have them going strong in minutes.

Three other pieces of equipment for ultralight trail cooking are worth mentioning. One is a wire finger-hole saw. Generally intended for use in survival kits, these saws average about 15 inches in length and consist of a wire containing hundreds of tiny cutting edges. A metal ring at each end allows you to pull the saw back and forth during the cutting operation. One of these gadgets weighs less than $1/2$ ounce and can be tucked inconspicuously in the pack.

Another idea is to use a folding knife that in place of one of the blades has a small saw. I really like these combination saw/knives because they do the job with little effort and serve double-duty if the outing is a big-game hunt and some bone cutting is necessary before packing out an animal.

Wire finger-hole saws are extremely lightweight and just the ticket for reducing wood to cooking size.

Finally, in Chapter 8, I mentioned the importance of having some type of small shovel or entrenching tool for preparing the fire site, restoring it to its natural appearance before leaving, and moving coals around in the fire pit while cooking. A small shovel also is necessary for burying non-burnable refuse, yet since any of the conventional designs trail cooks often use are much too heavy for ultralight work, why not consider a special backpacking trowel? These are

Instead of a full-size entrenching tool, consider the ultralight trowel shown here for use around the fire site.

made of hard plastic and look almost like metal trowels used for gardening. They weigh about 4½ ounces and are available in most camping-supply stores.

ULTRALIGHT TRAIL STOVES

Certain types of trail stoves are better suited to ultralight camping than others. Right off, eliminate those fueled by bulky, heavy butane or propane canisters. Kerosene trail stoves, as well, are heavier than those that use unleaded gasoline, white gasoline, Coleman fuel, or alcohol.

The Svea 123UR is an excellent example of an ultralight trail stove. Weighing a scant 12 ounces, it will bring a small pot of water to a boil in only six minutes. The thing I especially like about this particular model, and others similar to it, is that its protective housing doubles as a small kettle with a detachable handle. If he is willing to cook individual items in a meal one by one and eat them separately, a 'packer can make this stove and his utensils the entire extent of his cooking and eating gear.

In addition to the Svea 123UR, other popular, lightweight stoves include the 18-ounce Svea 123R and the 16-ounce Mountain Safety Research (MSR) model. All three use gasoline or an equivalent substitute such as Coleman fuel.

The lightest trail stove made today is the Trangia 25, which burns alcohol and comes in at a featherweight 3.5 ounces. However, this stove does not burn nearly as hot as the gasoline models (no alcohol stoves do), so its owner should choose menu items compatible with its use (such as foods that need only to be warmed or gently simmered, as compared to those that require a continuous, rolling boil).

Still other stoves are available to fill the bill, but whether you decide on a gasoline or an alcohol model, you can pare still more weight by carefully determining how much fuel

A splendid example of an ultralight trail stove is the Svea 123UR, which weighs a scant 12 ounces and comes housed in its own pot.

you need and then packing only that amount in a fuel flask or bottle no larger than is necessary. This is a relatively easy task. In Chapter 9, I gave a cross-comparison chart of popular stoves, including the approximate length of time it takes each one to bring an 8-ounce pan of water to a boil. The chart also gives the fuel capacity of each stove and the approximate burning time. With these figures, plus the required cooking time stated on packages of freeze-dried backpacking foods, or in other recipes, it is not a brow-furrowing proposition to determine almost to the ounce how much fuel is required for an entire outing of any duration.

For example, let's say you are preparing a lunch menu with the specific items that have to be cooked, consisting of Mountain House Freeze-Dried Beef Stroganoff with Noodles, along with a side dish of Mountain House Freeze Dried Peas. Suppose you are using the Svea 123UR white-gas stove, which has a fuel capacity of 6 ounces, burns for a total of sixty minutes on that quantity of fuel, and brings an 8-ounce pan of water to a boil in six minutes. The directions on the food packages require 8 ounces of boiling water to reconstitute each dish. That gives a required total of twelve minutes of fuel-consumption time. A bit of long division will tell you that you need 2 ounces of fuel to prepare this particular meal. Then, all you have to do is similarly calculate the fuel requirements for the other meals during the outing, add perhaps an ounce or two for good measure (or for the priming agent required for certain stoves) and take only that amount.

If it seems on the surface that carefully measuring such fuel quantities is overly picky, keep in mind white gasoline weighs close to 2½ pounds per quart (including the container).

Other lightweight stoves. Two additional types of stoves perfect for lightweight trail cooking have been reserved for special mention in this chapter. The first is the Sterno Piggyback Stove made by the Colgate-Palmolive Com-

Sterno canned heat is popular, but the heat output is not high. Therefore, the fuel is useful for cooking only those foods that require low heat.

The Sterno Piggyback Stove weighs only 7½ ounces, which includes a fuel supply that will last several hours.

pany. This little beauty utilizes Sterno Canned Heat cooking fuel, a type of jellied alcohol that is put up in a very lightweight aluminum can with a snap-top lid. Lighting the stove in any weather condition is as easy as prying off the lid and touching a match to the contents.

The "stove" part of the assemblage is a lightweight aluminum collar that, during storage and transportation, fits snuggly around the fuel can's diameter. To use, remove the stove collar from the can, turn it upside-down, then slide it back over the top of the can, where dimples on the inside of the aluminum hold the stove securely in place about $1\frac{1}{2}$ inches above the flame. To turn the stove off after use, you need only replace the lid. Wait a few minutes for the can to cool before putting it back in your pack. The Sterno Piggyback Stove and accompanying fuel can weigh only $7\frac{1}{2}$ ounces; the fuel burns for approximately two-and-a-half hours.

Another ultralight trail stove is one you can make yourself at no cost. Take a medium-size tin can that has had only one end removed and along the bottom edge of the open end use tin snips to cut out a small, rectangular opening to serve as a fire door. At the still-intact end of the can, use a can opener to punch out five or six holes around the can's diameter near the top rim, then punch out several more holes on the top surface of the lid. The stove is now ready to use. A slight variation of this: instead of using a beer can opener, merely make a number of $\frac{1}{4}$-inch holes with an electric drill through the top of the can and around the sides near the top rim.

To use, build a small fire no larger than your fist from twigs, branch tips, and other dry woods $\frac{1}{4}$ to $\frac{1}{2}$ inch in diameter and only a couple of inches long. Have an additional supply of the same-size wood on hand. Although this fire can be built directly on the ground, I generally like to prepare it on a large flat rock.

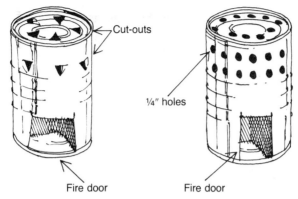

These tin-can stoves cost nothing more than ten minutes of your time. They are ideal for use in windy weather, and heat output is every high even with minimal fuel because of the efficient draft that is created.

When the fire is going well, stand your tin can stove upright on top of the fire, entirely enclosing it, with the fire door, of course, at the bottom. You now can set a small frypan or pot on top of the can's makeshift burner. Periodically add more wood, if necessary, to the fire by inserting a few additional sticks at a time through the fire door.

This little stove is a dandy. It weighs only an ounce or two, costs absolutely nothing other than the ten minutes it takes to make, and does a dandy job, especially in very windy weather when almost any other kind of open fire would be dangerous or difficult to manage. Furthermore, even though only a modest amount of kindling is required, the stove burns very hot because it operates on the same principle as a chimney with an efficient draft mechanism.

One of these little stoves will last many outings. However, it becomes very soot-blackened, so it's a good idea to store and transport it in some type of homemade cloth bag.

COOKING GEAR AND
UTENSILS

Much of the cooking gear described in Chapter 10 is entirely suitable for ultralight use, particularly the one-man aluminum cook kits made by companies such as Palco, Mirro, and Optimus. (The venerable Army mess kit, by comparison, is a mite on the heavy side because it's made from stamped sheet metal.) I usually remove the plastic drinking cup that comes in most one-man cooking kits and substitute an aluminum Sierra cup, which hangs from a thong on the outside of my pack. The Sierra cup, a bit larger than an ordinary cook-kit coffee cup, is convenient for preparing an individual serving of soup, stew, or even side dishes such as vegetables or pudding. The metal cup can be heated on a stove or over a fire, while the plastic types cannot.

A cast-iron dutch oven or an aluminum sheet-metal reflector oven is an impossibility in ultralight trail tramping. Happily, though, the Optimus-Princess Company, the leading Swedish manufacturer of compact, lightweight trail stoves, has come to the rescue of trail breads, muffins, and pies with the recent introduction of an ultralight oven. Called the Mini-Oven Model 334, this ingenious device is superb for concocting all manner of baked goods. The unit is 9 inches in diameter, 3¾ inches high, and weighs just 15 ounces (compare that to 15 *pounds* for a cast-iron dutch oven). It consists of three parts—a black sheet-metal bottom, an enameled oven dish, and a vented aluminum cover with a recessed knob—that nest together for use over a trail-stove burner, tin-can stove, or small fire.

I recommend using any of the biscuit, cake, muffin or bread recipes given in earlier chapters, scaled down to one-man or two-man portions. When you buy such an oven you also get a booklet of recipes.

This ultralight one-person mess kit by Palco is a serviceable unit. The author substitutes a metal Sierra cup for the plastic one in the kit, and dislikes the bolt-nut assembly on that frypan handle, which could accidently get lost.

The deep-dish bowls in this one-person kit by Optimus can be used for eating or mixing. Special pot-grabber utensil allows pan, bowls, and kettle to be used on a stove or over a fire. You may wish to substitute a Sierra cup for the plastic one in the kit.

An ultralight solution to a heavy cast-iron dutch oven or a reflector oven is the Mini-Oven by Optimus. It consists of an enameled oven dish, a vented aluminum cover, and a sheet-metal bottom. Weight: only 15 ounces.

There are numerous ways to approach the subject of eating utensils. Many backpacking purists (the ones who cut the handles off their toothbrushes to save $^3/_{16}$ of an ounce) stalwartly insist nothing other than a spoon is required for all eating activities.

Maybe so. But somehow, eating certain foods, such as fried eggs, mashed potatoes, or gravy with a spoon seems to me wholly unnatural and only one notch above eating with your hands alone. Go ahead and attack your chicken stew, chili, or beans and franks with a spoon, but in my mind more elegant repasts such as shrimp creole, beef almondine, beef ramen, and tuna à la neptune deserve better. For these, I usually pack a fork (which performs chores other than eating, such as turning meat) and use my pearl-handled pocket-knife for occasional cutting. The added half ounce a fork weighs can't be *that* critical.

For those who disagree, consider two alternatives: the "forkspoon," a regular spoon with the cut-off tine section of a fork soldered to the spoon's handle (you can make it in your home workshop in five minutes), or a Swiss Army Knife, a utilitarian piece of equipment that serves countless needs. Models range from those with only four accessory tools to some veritable monsters sporting more than fifteen. A few of the tools commonly housed are assorted knife blades, fork, spoon, pliers, scissors, adjustable wrench, screwdriver, awl, leather punch, nail file, nail clippers, and small saw blade.

The only twinge of uneasiness I have toward the Swiss Army Knife is that if you depend on it for all your tools and

Manufacturers have pared the weights of cook kits by eliminating handles and wire bails. Instead, use a pair of pot-grabber pliers, a useful, inexpensive addition to your gear.

When you can't afford the extra weight of a Swedish saw
but need to cut wood and dress big-game animals, a knife
with a saw blade is just the ticket.

utensils, and it should become lost during an outing, you
may find yourself in a real fix, or at best greatly inconvenienced. When you use separate tools and utensils, the loss of
any particular item, while lamented, can at least be compen-
sated for through the "make do" use of something else.

COOKING TIPS

Ultralight trail cooking, by its very description, must in-
volve the almost exclusive use of freeze-dried backpack
foods (or homemade recipes using dehydrated foods). No
rationale can be made for foods in cans, tins, jars, plastic
bottles, or other heavy containers. Nor can any allowance
be made for fresh meats, fruits, vegetables, eggs, and the
like — other than wild edibles that may be gathered along the
way or the happy occasion when fish or game can be taken.
Further, the remaining food choices must have a bare
minimum of water or moisture content because this com-

prises the bulk weight of all foods in their natural states. Which brings us full circle: Eliminating any food's water content, or at least appreciably reducing it, can be accomplished only through modern factory freeze-drying, commercial dehydration techniques, or home-drying methods.

Certain categories of freeze-dried backpack foods, or those which are dehydrated, however, are distinctly more advantageous than others. The crucial element is the "swell factor," a term I coined several years ago; it has to do with the expanded, reconstituted size of any given ready-to-eat meal as compared to its packaged weight in freeze-dried or dehydrated form. The ideal lightweight trail food can be reduced to minimal dry weight, yet through the addition of water be transformed into a maximum quantity of edible food, retaining all the essential nutrients of that food.

Foods which have the highest swell factors are the starchy carbohydrates, followed by high-protein foods. Fats, as a category, generally have the lowest swell factors. Examples of carbohydrate foods with high swell factors are rice, noodles, spaghetti, potatoes, and baked goods such as breads and biscuits. These (with the exception of the baked goods, which you make yourself) also are predominently the most flavorful of the freeze-dried offerings from backpack food companies. And because they are so high in carbohydrates, they offer the peak energy levels so important to active trail trampers, and should comprise at least fifty percent of their daily total gram intake.

Numerous companies offer virtually hundreds of freeze-dried and/or dehydrated menu items, and it would be a ponderous task to try and list even a fraction of them. But following is a random selection of ones I've personally tried and found to be tasty, high in carbohydrate content, high in swell factor, and, hence, ideal choices for those traveling ultralight.

Mountain House Brand (from Oregon Freeze Dry Foods)

Beef and Rice with Onions
Rice and Chicken
Potatoes and Beef
Noodles and Chicken
Spaghetti with Meat Sauce
Beef Stroganoff
Lasagna with Meat Sauce

Potato Casserole
Macaroni and Cheese
Buttermilk Pancakes
Corn
Chicken Noodle Soup
Banana Cream Pudding

Rich-Moor Corporation

Beef Stroganoff
Chicken a la Rice
Noodle-Turkey Dinner
Macaroni and Cheese
Stack-of-Cakes
Rice and Beef
Noodle Dinner with Beef

Pizza Dinner
Italian Spaghetti
Potato-Ham Dinner
Ranch Style Breakfast
Spuds and Beef
Rice-Vegetable Dinner

Tea Kettle Brand (from Recreational Equipment, Inc.)

Chicken with Rice

Dri-Lite Backpacker's Pantry
(from Recreational Equipment, Inc.)

Buttermilk Pancake Mix
Beef Stromboli with Rice
Creamed Chicken with Noodles

Compressed, freeze-dried foods are ideal when both weight and space are crucial. Each of these green-bean "tablets" will expand to yield five half-cup servings.

The Oregon Freeze Dry Foods Company now has freeze-dried foods compressed into small discs or tablets available under the trade name Space Savors (mentioned in Chapter 2). These incredibly advanced foods are the ultimate in lightweight-food technology. Following are the items presently available from the Oregon-based firm; by the time you read this, there are certain to be many more.

Vegetables	Net weight dry (ounces)	Reconstituted servings
Green peas	4.5	6 ½-cup portions
Green beans	1.6	5 ½-cup portions
Corn	4.9	5 ½-cup portions
Meats		
Cooked Diced Beef	2.3	2 6-oz. portions
Cooked Diced Chicken	2.3	2 6-oz. portions
Main-course entrees		
Beef and rice with onions	5.4	2 10-oz. portions
Chili with beans	6.8	2 10-oz. portions
Vegetable stew with beef	3.8	2 10-oz. portions
Rice and chicken	5.5	2 10-oz. portions
Shrimp creole	4.2	2 10-oz. portions
Beef-flavored rice	5.0	2 10-oz. portions

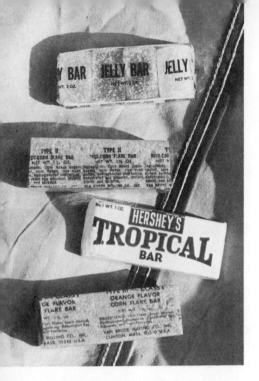

Quick-energy foods in concentrated form are high in
carbohydrates and favorites
with ultralight travelers.

Although not freeze-dried, numerous other specialty
foods offered by the backpacking supply companies are
worth mentioning briefly. One of my favorite snack items is
Hershey's Tropical Bars, highly concentrated energy
foods. Several types of high-carbohydrate bars, such as
rice-corn bars and orange- or lemon-flavored cornflake
bars, are also available. Consider, as well, the many types
of high-sugar candies. All of these are specially designed to
have high melt points so they can be carried in your pockets
even on the warmest days.

Dried meats such as bacon bars and meat bars also are
great for trail munching, accompaniments to meals, or even
broken into pieces and added to soups and stews. Homemade jerky goes at the top of the list (see Chapter 4).

One extraordinarily simple meal I often enjoy is a hearty,
nutritious jerky-rice casserole:

254

Jerky-Rice Casserole

1 cup Minute rice
1 teaspoon margarine or butter
8 jerky sticks, broken
1 cup water

Most rice recipes require a small quantity of salt, but since the jerky already is salty none is recommended here. At home, measure the rice into a small plastic bag and secure with a twist-tie. On the trail, bring the water to a boil, reduce the heat slightly, add the jerky pieces, and let simmer for 5 minutes. Then stir in the rice and margarine, cover the pan, remove from the heat, and let stand for 5 more minutes, fluffing occasionally. Serves two.

This meal can be varied in numerous ways. Substitute dried egg noodles for the rice, or a crumbled bacon bar or meat bar for the jerky. Add a teaspoon of dried tomato flakes, or a teaspoon of dried onion flakes. Better yet, after you've brought the water to a boil, dissolve a beef bouillon cube in the cauldron before adding the jerky and rice. To make a sumptuous casserole, add a dry instant-vegetable-soup mix to the boiling water before slipping in the rice and jerky (remember to increase the water in the recipe by whatever amount is required to reconstitute the vegetable soup).

These additions (soup mix, tomato flakes, onion flakes, or similar ingredients) can be packaged in tiny, labeled plastic bags all housed in one slightly larger bag. Or browse through any backpacking retail outlet for plastic canisters with snap-top lids. These assorted little vessels, which hold quantities ranging anywhere from one teaspoon to one-half

Jerky is a superb food for lightweight cooking. Slice chunks into broth for a hearty soup. Dried jerky will absorb moisture and swell into tender, juicy pieces of meat.

cup, are ideal for transporting loose ingredients such as tea, coffee, or sugar. Our old friend the 35mm film canister must once more be recommended as one of the best things to serve 'packers since the invention of the knapsack.

Beef and chicken bouillon cubes, although they have no nutritional value, can improve the taste of high-carbohydrate, rice or noodle meals. You can dissolve a bouillon cube in hot water in the usual manner, stir in just a pinch of flour or cornstarch to make a gravy, and pour it over noodles or reconstituted potatoes or meats. Or, when the bouillon cube is dissolved, stir in a tablespoon or two of Cream of Wheat, Cream of Rice, or wheat germ to create a thick cereal-like dish.

For frying—pancakes or fresh fish, if instance—take along a tiny plastic bottle of Vegelene, made by the Rich-Moor Food Corporation (order it by mail from the address in Appendix 1, if it's not available from your local supplier).

For transporting small quantities of loose foods, spices, and sea-sonings, consider the many vials and tubes available from back-packing supply stores. All have moistureproof snap-top lids. Our old friend, the 35mm canister, serves the purpose well, too.

Bouillon cubes have limitless uses—for hot beverages, flavorful additions to noodle dishes, or making gravy. Each cube weighs only one-third ounce and makes 1 cup of broth.

Cooking oil is too heavy for ultralight trail tramping. Instead, use highly concentrated Vegelene, made by Rich-Moor. Just a tiny bit is needed to fry foods.

Vegelene is a highly concentrated, polyunsaturated vegetable oil intentionally designed for trail cooking. Because of its concentrated form, far less is required for pan frying than with ordinary cooking oils. It is also designed to withstand the erratic frying temperatures of open-fire cooking and thereby reduces sticking or burning.

The stuff is expensive (about a dollar for a 1-ounce plastic squeeze bottle, which makes it cost about ten times more than an equivalent amount of Crisco or Wesson Oil), but nothing is better, and one bottle used under normal circumstances should last through several outings.

RECIPES

Here is a pot pourri of recipes we rate highly for ultralight trail cooking. In many cases, the majority of ingredients can be weighed or measured and then prepackaged at home in plastic bags (label the contents of each bag and enclose a slip of paper stating additional ingredients that must be added later and cooking instructions).

Super Omelet

> **2 oz. dehydrated egg**
> **1 oz. dry milk powder**
> **¼ oz. dried mushrooms**
> **¼ oz. dehydrated green pepper**
> **¼ oz. dried onion flakes**
> **1 oz. dry cheddar-cheese food**

At home, prepackage items separately in tiny plastic bags, then place all in one larger bag that is clearly labeled. In camp, place onions, mushrooms, and peppers in one cup water and let stand 15 minutes. When reconstituted, mix in egg powder and dried milk to form a batter (add just a bit more water if batter seems too thick). Pour onto greased frypan and cook without stirring for about 3 minutes. Sprinkle cheese over left half of omelet, then carefully fold right half over to cover. Place lid on pan and let cook three more minutes until done and cheese is melted. Season lightly with salt and pepper. Serves two.

Vegetable-Rice Medley

> **1 cup Minute rice**
> **¼ teaspoon salt**
> **1 oz. dried mushrooms**
> **2 oz. dehydrated mixed vegetables**
> **1 packet beef-gravy mix**

Prepackage items separately (except mushrooms and vegetables, which can be mixed). Bring one cup of water and the salt to a boil, stir in rice, cover the pan and set aside for 5 minutes. In a second container, mix the vegetables and gravy in 2 cups water, bring to a boil, then quickly reduce heat and simmer until vegetables are soft (about 5 minutes). Pour gravy-vegetables mix over rice. Serves two.

Hearty Beef Soup

1 envelope instant beef-soup mix
1 oz. dehydrated mixed vegetables
1 oz. dehydrated green beans
1 beef bouillon cube
1 oz. dried beef or jerky
2 oz. grated Parmesan cheese or seasoned croutons

Prepackage ingredients (except vegetables) separately. In a pan bring 5 cups of water to a rolling boil, stir in all ingredients except cheese or croutons, reduce heat, cover, and slowly simmer 15 minutes. Just before serving, sprinkle Parmesan cheese or seasoned croutons over top of soup. Serves two.

John's Favorite Dumplings

2 eggs (dry-powder equivalent)
1 tablespoon salt
1 cup flour

Prepackage items separately. In camp, reconstitute eggs by adding water called for on envelope. Then add more water to double the volume. Stir until thoroughly mixed. Then stir in just enough flour to make a medium-thin dough. In a kettle, add the salt to 2 quarts of water. When the water reaches a rapid boil, hold the bowl of dough over the kettle and with a spoon cut off dumplings (golf-ball size) and let them fall into the cauldron. As soon as the dough hits the hot water it will swell up into tender dumplings, but cover the pot, turn down the heat, and let them simmer for about two or three minutes. These dumplings are outstanding served with gravy over them, or "floated" in bowls of soup or stew. Serves two.

Beef Stroganoff and Noodles

4 oz. dried beef
1 envelope beef-stroganoff-sauce mix
½ oz. dried mushrooms
1 envelope dry sour-cream mix
3 tablespoons dry powdered milk
6 oz. wide noodles

Prepackage items in separate plastic bags, then all in one larger bag with label and instructions. In camp, add ½ cup water to the sour-cream mix, stir, and set aside for ten minutes. Bring 2 quarts lightly salted water to a boil for the noodles. Reconstitute the beef with one cup of water, then remove, cut into cubes and brown in a frypan with a small amount of oil. Add stroganoff sauce and mushrooms to the pan the meat is in and ½ cup water, and blend until smooth. Simmer uncovered for 5 minutes and then stir in the sour-cream sauce. Cook noodles 8 to 10 minutes, drain, and pour the meat and sauce over the noodles. Serves two hungry hikers.

Sausage Goulash

4 oz. dried potato buds or slices
6 oz. dried sausage
2 tablespoons cooking oil
1 teaspoon dried onion flakes
¼ teaspoon dried tomato flakes
1 envelope dry tomato-soup mix

Prepackage items separately in small plastic bags, then all in one larger bag that is labeled, with cooking instructions. In camp, cut dry sausage sticks into pieces and brown in cooking oil in frypan. Reconstitute dried potatoes in bowl with water per instructions on package. Add 2 cups water to frypan, stir in onion flakes, tomato flakes, and tomato-soup mix. Stir thoroughly and then let simmer on low heat for 5 minutes or until dried foods are reconstituted. Drain any water from potatoes, add to frypan, stir, cover and let simmer 5 minutes longer. Serves two.

16

Survival Cooking

I'll admit I have never found myself in an authentic life-or-death survival situation. I credit it to Explorer Scout activities I participated in as a youth and then later survival-school training exercises during a military stint at Fort Benning, Georgia. Both experiences taught me how to tap the abundance of food, water, and shelter possibilities available in the wilds. Perhaps even more important, they showed me the importance of advance planning to ward off the likelihood of finding in that dire a predicament in the first place.

Consequently, I strongly believe every serious outdoorsman who likes to roam off the beaten path should make a point of signing up for some type of survival class. Local agencies, schools, or other organizations occasionally conduct wilderness survival classes for the general public for a modest enrollment fee. Survival training is also offered through Outward Bound (384 Field Point Road, Greenwich, Connecticut 06830), Red Cross or Civil Defense groups, but Boy Scout, Girl Scout, YMCA, YWCA, and other local clubs sometimes conduct them as well. Worth investigating, too, are two-year junior colleges, community colleges, and technical schools that have forestry, fish-and game-management, outdoor-recreation, or natural-resource curriculums because they frequently offer survival classes. If you should sign up for military service, you'll get the most extensive survival training available—for free.

In outdoor-survival classes, students attend evening classes in which they view slides or films and listen to lectures by respected authorities on virtually all aspects of survival. On brief field trips, the class, led by an instructor, actually constructs various types of shelters, locates water, starts fires, gathers edible foods, and much more, Finally, the students take a type of "final exam" that pits individuals alone against the elements for a two- or three-day weekend in which they must fend for themselves with a bare amount of rations and equipment.

There are also a number of excellent books on the market that are worth studying. One I can highly recommend is Byron Dalrymple's *Survival in the Outdoors,* E. P. Dutton, $6.95, available at bookstoores or from the Outdoor Life Book Club, P.O. Box 2016, Latham, New York 12111. Another invaluable guide is the *Search and Rescue Survival Manual,* from the Department of the Air Force, HQ, USAF, Washington, D.C. 20330. Both works are extremely detailed in all facets of survival, whereas in this chapter I will only be looking at basic survival-cooking techniques.

Webster defines "survival" as the struggle for existence. It is logical, then, that survival cooking has to do with those emergency situations in which an outdoorsman is faced with the task of acquiring sufficient food and water to sustain life functions. Fortunately, barring a major calamity such as a light plane crash, falling off a cliff and incurring serious injury, or losing all of your gear and provisions in a

raging wilderness river, it is actually quite rare to find yourself in a real life-or-death situation. What many sportsmen
more commonly find themselves confronted with are temporary periods of inconvenience or uncomfortable hardship
with no real threat to survival.

Take the fall of 1980 when an unexpected blizzard
dumped an incredible four feet of snow on the region surrounding Glenwood Springs, Colorado. Hundreds of hunters who had packed into the high country for mule deer and
elk suddenly found themselves stranded. A local Army
Corps of Engineers detachment began airlifting hunters out
with helicopters, but many of those stranded had little alternative but wait until the low-flying search-and-rescue missions found them. For some, the wait was as long as four or
five days. Those who were in established tent camps when
the storm struck simply bided their time, though food
supplies were running precariously low. Others who were
away from camp hunting when the blizzard hit were forced
to contrive makeshift shelters such as snow caves and live
on whatever meager rations they happened to have in their
coat pockets.

Every year countless trail trampers simply become lost
and must stay put until authorities organize search parties.
This can mean making do for perhaps as long as a week.
As a precaution, always tell somebody the direction you're
heading, your anticipated destination, and your estimated
time of return. If you become hopelessly lost, don't continue to wander randomly; that will make the task of finding
you all the more difficult. Build a fire and stay in one place.

Once I backpacked into Idaho's Bitterroot Range on a
routine outing to photograph sheep and found myself temporarily lost. Although I had been there before and knew
the exact route I decided to explore a small alpine lake I
had never noticed before on my topographical map. It was
only three miles off my planned itinerary, I figured, and I

would intercept my usual route out farther ahead. A winding canyon with many side corridors confused me, however, and I took a wrong turn that cost me an extra two days of hiking — with no food — to get back where I was supposed to be. Not a life-or-death situation, but I admit I was shaken when I realized I'd have to fend for myself for two days.

You may intentionally choose to test your ingenuity at mild-mannered survival tactics in nonsurvival situations. If for no other reason, you have the self-satisfaction of learning new skills that could come in handy in the future.

BE PREPARED

The secret to surviving an emergency in the wilderness, or simply sweating out a time of great inconvenience, hinges primarily on being prepared for such eventualities well in advance of their occurrence. The preparation is twofold: First, you have to be mentally equipped, which entails not only a sound frame of mind but a working knowledge of what the human body requires in the way of periodic sustenance. Second, you should have survival equipment on your person at all times (and a good deal of wood's savvy in the event the bulk of this equipment is lost).

Depending on their physical and mental condition, and the type of terrain and climate they are exposed to, human beings can survive quite a long time without food. In 1962 an Indian Buddha, fasting in protest of political corruption, reportedly subsisted upon nothing but water for eight-one consecutive days and survived. In 1973, bush pilot Nelson Gary was returning after shuttling hunters to a camp in Manitoba's wilderness when his light plane crashed. After forty-two days of living on water and assorted wild greens we was rescued, none the worse for wear and tear, although 25 pounds lighter. Nine-year-old Kevin Dye made national headlines in 1974 when he was on his own for eleven days in Wyomings rugged Casper Mountain Range before being found by rescuers. The youth, slightly mentally retarded and a victim of epilepsy, survived.

These are extreme examples of deprivation, to be sure, but they confirm the fact, as do hundreds of other recorded cases, that the human body stands up remarkably well in the face of adverse conditions. Anyone who is lost or stranded for ten days or less need only keep in mind that, as unpleasant as it may be, the body can easily go for several weeks without refueling with no long-term effects. With the supplement of a few spartan rations and miscellaneous items foraged from the land, someone could conceivably survive for several months before being rescued. Precisely how long a person can exist without food is impossible to say. Too many variables enter the picture: When did the person last eat? What and how much? In what type of climate must the individual survive? What type of clothing is he wearing? What type of shelter is he able to construct from available materials? What type and amount of physical activity is required of him?

Bodily food requirements. When faced with a potential survival situation, it helps to know that the act of going without food progresses along very specific cause-and-effect lines. After several hours without food, the body begins absorbing itself in a type of self-cannibalization process. First, it begins consuming carbohydrates, and when those are largely depleted the fats begin to disappear. These initial two steps may take weeks and up to a certain point, for many of us who have lived sedentary lifestyles, such losses may not be all bad. Occasional headaches, fatigue, and acute hunger pangs may be the only unpleasant side effects. The problem begins to intensify and near the critical stage, however, when the bulk of the body's carbohydrates and fat reserves are greatly diminished; that's when our internal furnaces begin to consume proteins in the form of muscle tissue and tendons. The symptoms of food deprivation now begin to reveal themselves in the form of dried and discolored skin, skin eruptions, cuts that refuse to heal, severe cramps, a sharp drop in blood pressure and pulse rate, the inability to think rationally.

Hence, any food source should be considered very welcome in survival situations. But if a choice can be made (and it likely can), it is best to first satisfy the body's continually ongoing needs for energy-producing carbohydrates and fats, with a lesser emphasis devoted to the acquisition of proteins.

Water requirements. The human body's need for water is far more stringent and well-defined than it is for food. Depending on the climate and degree of physical exertion, survival without water can be measured in terms of days or even hours. Naturally, the hotter and drier the climate, the greater the body's need for water to replace that lost through perspiration. Under optimum conditions in which the climate is cool and the individual is greatly restricting his level of activity, it is possible to live without fluid replacement for as long as five or six days. Yet in the desert heat of 120°F survival time without water and shelter from the blistering sun can be less than forty-eight hours.

It stands to reason, then, that water should go at the head of a list of prerequisites for survival, followed by shelter (or fire, or adequate clothing) in a less than hospitable environment, and finally food.

Review the suggestions in Chapter 7 for finding and purifying water, and remember these tips, as well, for locating emergency water sources:

• In extremely arid country, look for cactus species, particularly the saguaro and barrel varieties. These plants store water like camels and when sliced open, the inner pulp can be mashed against itself and a resulting liquid squeezed out.

- Fresh water can often be obtained on the beaches of saltwater ocean fronts by understanding the physical principle of specific gravity. Saltwater is much heavier than sweetwater and consequently occupies lower strata levels in subsurface beach areas. Find a place about five yards inland from the low-tide mark and begin digging with your hands until just a tiny bit of seepage begins to trickle into the hole in the sand, then dig no deeper. Wet a finger with the water and test it, and likely you'll find it to be fresh. The trick is to dig no deeper than absolutely necessary, or deeper lying saltwater will then begin to fill the hole and contaminate the fresh.

- If it is raining but you have no container in which to collect the water, take off your absorbent cotton T-shirt and hang it from a tree branch. It will soak up the precipitation like a sponge, allowing you to periodically wring out a steady stream of water into your mouth.

Food and water intake. It's important also to mention the interplay between food and water intake in a survival situation. It is wise to ration any amount of available food over a moderate period of time. This is not the case with water since the continued function of bodily systems requires that water lost through perspiration be replenished as quickly as possible (not by drinking excessive amounts, however). Avoiding perspiration is one way to reduce the body's loss of essential water stores; therefore, in warm weather avoid physical activity, remain in shaded places, and if you must travel or move around, do so at night when the air temperature is much cooler. Also, eating any food requires the body to use water during the course of digestion; hence, if your water supply is critically low, one means of conservation is not eating.

It is crucial, too, to consider specific types of foods available for eating. Bland foods that are high in moisture content are the most desirable, especially foods that have not been dehydrated or freeze-dried. Conversely, foods that are dry and starchy, and also meats, not only have a tendency to increase thirst but also require more water in the act of digestion, as do foods containing a lot of salt or other pungent or spicy seasonings. As a result, if all you have are highly seasoned, dry foods, it is much better to avoid eating altogether than to further aggravate your already acute water-shortage problem.

Finally, when there is a shortage of water, don't consume any alcoholic beverages that you may have; alcohol is an astringent that dehydrates body tissues while simultaneously increasing thirst. Smoking tobacco also causes a dry throat and increases thirst, yet chewing tobacco activates saliva flow to keep the mouth moist and reduce thirst.

SURVIVAL EQUIPMENT

The responsible sportsman carries a pocketknife or sheath knife, a waterproof matchcase in his pocket, and a compass hanging from his belt on a leather thong or pinned to the front of his jacket. These are three essentials no hunter, angler, or backwoods roamer should ever leave home without. Next on the agenda is a survival kit. It should be so small, lightweight, and convenient that it stays unobtrusively in your pocket until needed. This is where many so-called survival kits fall short: they are either too large and heavy to fit into a coat pocket and therefore are relegated to the pack—which serves no useful purpose if the pack is lost—or they are left home altogether. The most valuable survival kit in the world, no matter how modest the contents, is the one you have on your person at all times.

This small survival kit is no larger than a pack of cigarettes, yet contains essentials that are valuable for obtaining fish or game. Items include (1) concentrated jelly bar, (2) concentrated chocolate, (3) three bouillon cubes, (4) waterproof matches, (5) spool of heavy mono fishing line. (6) wire leader for toothy fish or turtles, (7) light mono line, (8) storage can, (9) turtle or big-fish hooks, (10) medium-size hooks, (11) plastic 1-quart water bag, (12) flies, (13) razor blade, (14) lures, (15) aluminum foil, (16) small hooks, (17) water-purification tablets.

The one I used is housed in a small Band-Aid can no larger than a pack of king-size cigarettes and weighs only 5 ounces. If the weather is warm, it even will ride in a buttoned-down shirt pocket.

After adding and subtracting numerous items over the years, I've settled upon these as best (you may want to make adjustments depending on the terrain, climate, or other conditions you most frequently encounter):

- A plastic 1-quart water bag that folds up into a tiny one-inch-square packet.

- Twelve Halazone tablets that have been removed from their original bottle and sealed in plastic to ensure they remain waterproof.
- Three different types of food — two types of high-energy candy bars (any others with high-carbohydrate content would be suitable) and beef or chicken bouillon cubes (when dissolved in hot water they yield three cups of flavorful soup). How do you make the soup?
- A small packet of heavy duty aluminum foil, which, unfolded, spreads out to 12 inches square. To make bouillon soup, simply fashion a cup by forming the foil around your fist, turning over the edges of the rim for strength, and placing it beside your fire. The foil has other uses as well: it will reflect light in the same manner as a signal mirror; it can be wrapped around a fish or other pieces of meat and buried in glowing coals to cook the food, then washed and reused again and again; if your hat is lost, the foil can be fashioned into a cap to reflect bright sunlight and keep you cooler, thus reducing body perspiration; in cold weather, use it as a liner inside your cap to reduce the amount of heat that ordinarily escapes the body through the head.
- Additional waterproff matches, in the event the matchcase in my pocket is lost.
- A single-edge razor blade, to replace my knife, if lost, for cleaning fish or game, or innumerable other chores.
- Two kinds of nylon fishing line — a plastic spool containing 50 yards of 30-pound-test line and a smaller hank of 20 yards of 8-pound-test monofilament.
- Two spoons or larger baited fishhooks and a leader.

Some may wish to include a spare compass, but I find this unnecessary because I always have two anyway — a large Silva compass that hangs from my belt, and a smaller model that pins to my front pocket, where I can glance at it regularly, even when both hands are occupied.

Catching fish.   The larger, 30-pound-test line could be used to lash shelter together, but its primary purpose is to catch big fish (with a spoon or fishhook). To cast such lures or bait, take a 12-inch-long stick and force it through the center hole of the line spool so the two are securely held together. Now hold the stick in one hand with the thumb of the same hand over the top of the spool and cast like an ordinary spinning rod, releasing thumb pressure at just the right time so the line pays off the spool. To retrieve the lure, pull the line in hand over hand while simultaneously winding it onto the spool for the next "cast."

Use the smaller, 8-pound line on smaller lakes or streams where only panfish or small trout exist. One end of a short section of the line can be tied to a willow branch and the other to a small baited hook or artificial fly. To find live bait, lift dead logs or rocks and gather grubs, worms, or insects. In winter, peel the bark from a dead, standing tree, and you'll likely find the larva cases of various insects.

To "cast" lures, slide spool over end of stick, then use like a spinning reel, retrieving the line by winding it back on spool. The device won't cast a lure far, but it works.

COOKING YOUR CATCH

Smaller specimens such as panfish and trout can be dressed whole, laid across the top of a green, forked stick and broiled over an open fire. When one side is done, carefully turn the fish over and cook the other side. Somewhat larger fish such as pike can also be dressed whole and then, using the same type of forked stick, skewered on the prongs and broiled over a fire. In this case, the stick will necessarily have to be a bit thicker to support the added weight of the larger fish, and since the cooking time will take longer you may wish to prop the stick over the flames with heavy rocks.

Another way to cook fish over an open fire without conventional pans or other utensils is the standing-stick broiling technique. Begin by selecting two green sticks about 2 feet long and peel the bark from them. Lay the sticks one on top of the other and lash them together at one end. Now, cut off the head of your fish and remove the gills, but otherwise leave the skin intact to hold the meat in place as it cooks and becomes tender. Next, split the fish lengthwise down the back and open it outward with the belly section serving as a type of hinge. After you remove the entrails, insert several other peeled green sticks in a horizontal position through the flesh to keep it spread apart. Then position the fish between the two long sticks and squeeze them together to hold the fillet-slab in place, lashing them securely. The sticks can then be thrust into the ground in an upright position before the flames, or laid directly over the flames with supporting rocks in place.

Similar to this method, but recommended for the very largest fish you may be lucky enough to catch, is plank broiling. This technique requires a freshly split section of log from a nonconiferous tree, plus a smaller stick to support the "plank" as it faces the fire in a propped upward position.

Dress your fish exactly as in the standing-stick method and then attach it flesh-side-out to the plank with pegs. The "pegging" trick is no more complicated than using your pocketknife to gouge small holes in the plank, whittling small pegs from green branches to fit the holes, then tapping them in place after they are skewered through the fish. Robust flames are required for plank broiling and it may be necessary to adjust the position of the plank occasionally so all portions of the fish are adequately exposed to the heat.

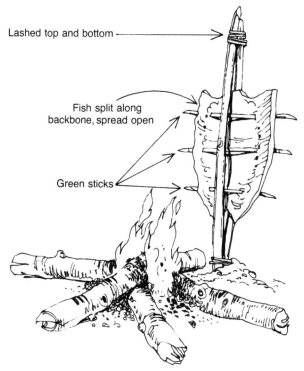

Lashed top and bottom

Fish split along backbone, spread open

Green sticks

An easy way to broil fish slabs without pans or utensils is the standing-stick method.

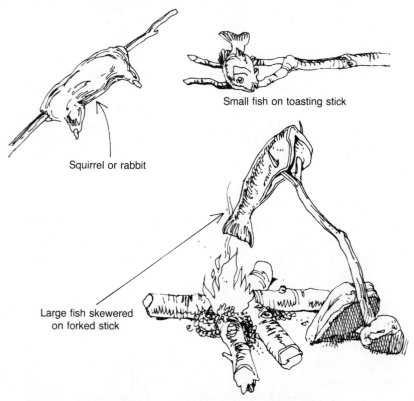

Squirrel or rabbit

Small fish on toasting stick

Large fish skewered on forked stick

Small fish and game can be skewered on sharp green sticks.

In all of the above situations, when the skin of the fish is golden brown and crispy and the meat flaky, it is ready to eat. You can do so with your fingers after the fish has cooled a bit.

If you have any trouble catching the fish, you'll want to salvage every last bit of edible meat or other valuable nutrients. To best do this, scale the fish and remove the innards and gills but not the head. Now cut the fish into chunks that will conveniently fit into whatever cooking vessel you have on hand (or your makeshift aluminum bowl).

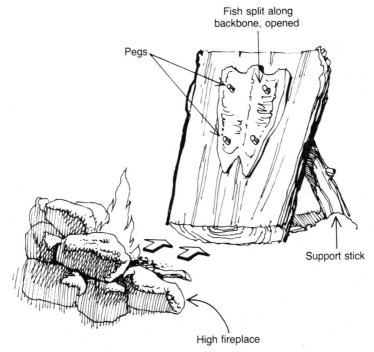

Plank-broiling is an easy way to cook large fish without imple-ments. The fish is held in place with whittled pegs pushed into holes gouged out with your knife.

Add water, bring to a boil over your fire, and cook gently until the fish is tender. When the meat has been eaten, you can drink the hearty broth flavored by the bones and remainder of the carcass.

Turtles. The wire leader in the survival kit can serve several purposes. If toothy fish such as pike are around, the leader can be tied to the terminal end of your nylon line to prevent bite-offs. It can also be fashioned into a snare for capturing small game animals (discussed later). But, mainly, the leader is for catching turtles. Tie a 10-foot length of the 30-

pound test mono line to some secure shoreline object, then tie the leader to the other end and place one of the larger hooks on the snap. Bait the hook with almost any type of carrion (dead fish) found along the shallow bank, toss the bait out, and by the following morning you should have a turtle to eat.

Kill the turtle by touching its nose with a stick; when the critter snaps at the stick and extends its neck to grab hold of it, lop off its head with a hand axe or knife.

The best way to cook a turtle in a survival situation (assuming you have lost all of your conventional cooking equipment) is first to cut along the sides to remove the shell where a thick cartilage joins the top and bottom halves. Then with your knife pluck out the meat located along the spine, skin out the meat on the neck and four legs, and boil the individual pieces in water (in your aluminum foil bowl) until tender. Drink the broth afterward. Or skewer small pieces of the turtle meat (the size of marshmallows) on a green stick and roast them one at a time over an open fire.

FORAGING FROM THE LAND

The outdoors is a repository of hundreds of plants and animals that can be eaten in genuine survival circumstances. Some of the foods are extremely tasty while others, due to our particular cultural biases, may literally have to be choked down. But when you think about the grisly alternative, the swallowing of such unseemly foods becomes remarkably easy.

The easiest foods to gather in the wild are plants and other vegetation because no hand-to-hand combat is necessary and, with their feet firmly rooted in the soil, there is no chance of their running away at your advance. For a refresher on the most commonly available edibles, look at the chapters "Wild Edible Plants" and "Nuts, Berries,

Fruits and Roots." Particularly valuable to survival eating are plants high in carbohydrate content, such as the starchy tuber plants like arrowhead and cattail. Next, priority should probably be given to berries, then nuts.

However, if plants cannot be positively identified, there are several ways to determine whether or not they are safe to eat:

- Foods you see being eaten by rodents (squirrels, lemmings, mice, opossums), bears, raccoons, badgers, and other omnivores usually are safe for humans, as well. Never trust birds, though; they often eat vegetation (as well as berries and fruits) that is poisonous to human beings.

- Avoid any plantlife that when broken yields a milky white juice. The exceptions are dandelions and wild lettuce.

- Do not eat plants that have a mottled or speckled appearance; they are probably diseased.

- Don't bother with mushrooms. Although you may be able to identify some kinds, none of the known species has any nutritive value.

- When in doubt as to whether a particular vegetative or plant species — or any other food for that matter — is safe to eat, take a small, pea-size portion and put it in your mouth for five minutes. If a slight burning sensation occurs or the food has a nauseating flavor or very bitter taste, spit it out and rinse your mouth because the food is probably unsafe to eat. If no such symptoms appear, swallow the tiny morsel and wait a full thirty minutes; virtually all malicious toxins manifest themselves within this time period. If you still feel no intestinal upset, eat two more pea-size portions and then wait a full twenty-four hours. After that, you can be relatively sure the food is safe to eat in at least moderate quantities.

If you have a seine, or can improvise one from a cloth shirt, you can capture small crustaceans. It takes a bit of effort, though.

Crayfish are highly nutritious and very tasty. Think of them as little lobsters; drop them into boiling water until their shells turn red.

Nuts, easily gathered in the fall, are extremely high in protein and make excellent survival foods.

Frog legs are a treat and highly nourishing. Although nimble hands may be able to grab an occasional frog, better results are obtained by fashioning a spear or gig from a long branch that is forked at one end.

Wild plants. It is best to eat varieties of wild greens and other vegetable matter raw because boiling them removes too many valuable vitamins and minerals. This also is a good practice when water is scarce. However, if water is abundant, and the plant in question (such as dandelions) is too bitter to eat raw, boil it several minutes, discard the water, boil a second time in fresh water, eat the tender, cooked plant, and then drink the water from the second boiling like a tea or thin vegetable soup.

The tubers (starchy root systems) of various plants can be eaten raw or may be peeled and then roasted on a flat, hot rock. Or toss them unpeeled into the hot ashes of a fire as you would a potato; when the outside is coal black, the tuber is cooked and may be extracted from the fire, peeled, and eaten with your fingers.

Berries. Many species of berries are plentiful across North America, and they are highly desirable food sources because they are high in sugar and moisture content. Yet they spoil easily in the warm temperatures during which they are most abundant, so don't pick large quantities at any one time. Eat them raw as you pick.

Nuts. Nuts are extremely high in proteins and fats and likewise should be highly sought after. All of the nuts described in Chapter 6 are quite nutritious, hickory nuts and acorns most of all. I didn't mention acorns previously because they have a very high tannin content that makes them very bitter when eaten raw. But in survival situations they are well worth gathering and if roasted near an open fire on a rock are almost palatable.

Bark. The bark from many species of trees is edible and in some cases highly nutritious. Pine bark, for example, is an excellent source of vitamin A. Other trees outdoorsmen are most likely to chance upon in the wilds include aspen, birch, basswood, willow, yellow (tulip) poplar, and cottonwood. Use your knife to scrape off the rough outer layer and then peel away thin strips of the inner layer and either chew it like jerky or boil it in water until soft.

BAGGING YOUR PREY

I already mentioned that catching fish and turtles is one of the easiest ways to obtain meat. Another way to catch fish is by spearing them from above with a gig fashioned from a long, lightweight sapling. With your knife, cut barbs or notches in the forked end of the stick to prevent a wiggling fish from escaping when impaled. Heat the forked end of the gig over a fire to harden the prongs.

The successful spear fisherman remains poised and motionless on an overhanging bank or rock outcropping until the moment is right for a quick downward jab of the gig. Remember the optical illusion caused by light refraction that causes a fish under the surface of the water to appear to be in a slightly different spot from where it really is; the trick is to aim the gig slightly to the rear of where the fish seems to be.

Frogs. The same gig used for fish also serves to spear frogs. Those big bulls that can be found sitting on the soft mud banks of a lake or river are much easier targets than those half submerged in the water. Use nearby tall bullrushes and other cover to conceal your stealthy approach. The hind legs of frogs deserve gourmet rating, but the front legs and back contain some edible meat, too. Simply cut off the legs, strip off the skin (a bit tedious but necessary and well worth the effort), then boil the meat or broil it over a small fire.

Crayfish. These "tiny lobsters" are a readily available food source in small streams, and their white flesh is difficult to distinguish from fresh shrimp. Crayfish are fast swimmers that require equally swift movements to capture them; they rapidly shoot backwards from one hiding place to another with quick thrusts of their abdomens and tails. The most efficient way to catch crayfish is a two-person operation. One person stands upstream and turns over rocks, while the other stands several yards downstream with a small seine net tied between two sticks to catch the crawdads as they are routed out and swept away by the current. If you don't have a seine net, carefully disassemble your T-shirt by removing the thread from the seams and making judicious cuts here and there to form a large square of porous material that can be tied between two sticks. If you don't have a partner, fashion a cup from your piece of aluminum foil, wade shallow, clear waters, and when you spot a crayfish quickly thrust the cup down to cover the critter and prevent its escape. Another easy way to catch crayfish is to find a steep rocky shoreline where the water is deep. Then tie a small piece of dead fish or other carrion to a length of fishing line and lower it to the bottom; when you feel a crayfish grab the offering slowly raise it to the surface and out of the water. (It won't let go.)

Crayfish are exceptionally high in protein, and preparing them is not complicated. Just drop them into boiling water until their shells turn from greenish brown to bright red, which signals they are done. Then, with your fingers, peel the tail section from the underneath side and extract the delicious white meat. With jumbo-size crayfish the front pincer claws also contain a worthwhile quantity of meat, but you'll need to cut the pincers open with your knife or crack them apart with rocks.

Freshwater clams and snails. These can be found in many bodies of water across the country. Boil them, then pry or break their shells apart, or eat them raw.

Insects. Equally nutritious are crickets, locusts, and grasshoppers. In fact, these are relished as special delicacies in the Middle East. The time to search for any of these insects is early in the morning or just before dusk when the coolness of the air makes them lethargic and the presence of dew causes them to climb to the tops of weed stems and other vegetation stalks. You can collect them by hand. Since the legs and wings are inedible immediately cut them off to prevent the insects from escaping.

The most convenient way to cook 'hoppers and other insects is by roasting them. Build a fire and in the middle place a flat rock until it becomes scorching hot. Then spread your assortment of insects on the rock and frequently turn them with a stick until they are crunchy brown. They are deliciously nutlike in flavor.

Snakes. Most species of snakes, even those with poisonous bites, make for fine eating when broiled. Capture them early in the morning or in the evening when the cool air has lowered their body metabolisms. Use a long, forked stick to pin a snake in the neck region firmly to the ground. Then give the snake a sharp rap across the head with a second stick. When the snake's skin is peeled away with your knife, sumptuous white meat lies beneath that many claim tastes very much like chicken or pork. It can be skewered in chunks on sharp sticks and roasted over glowing embers.

Big-game animals. No doubt, the hunter who finds himself in a survival situation will have some type of firearm in his possession. This makes felling larger animals relatively easy. Yet I am somewhat reluctant to recommend the killing of a big game animal such as a deer, moose, elk, or bear, unless one has reached the stage of dire circumstances and such an animal suddenly appears within easy range. For one, the vast quantity of meat on such large creatures is likely to spoil before it can be consumed entirely, unless the weather is cold enough to provide natural refrigeration. Also, an individual may later have to justify his action to authorities, most of whom are reasonable and fair-minded but may not agree that merely being lost for two days is cause for killing a cow elk or protected species such as a grizzly bear.

A much better decision, therefore, might be to concentrate on gamebirds, waterfowl, or small-game species that will adequately serve short-term needs, in conjunction with plants, nuts, fish, and other edibles. All of the game animals and birds residing in North America are edible, although some are not as palate pleasing as others. If you don't have a firearm, there are numerous other ways to capture them.

Small-game animals. A porcupine is one of the easiest animals to find and kill. Search for stands of pines or conifers where large patches of bark have been gnawed from the tree trunks; if you look carefully, you'll undoubtedly find the porcupine sitting on a branch somewhere or ambling along on the ground. If he's high up in a tree, shake the tree to dislodge him or knock him down with a poke from a long branch. Then, give the docile creature a rap over the head with a stout limb. To dress the animal, use your knife to open the belly region (where there are no quills) and peel the skin back on both sides so there is no danger of getting spiked. With the hide thusly removed, complete the field-dressing operation as you would with any other small-game animal.

You can kill beavers and muskrats the way you would a porcupine. The trick is to waylay them out of the water, on high, dry ground where their movements are awkward and slower.

Snares and deadfalls.   If all else fails, you can contrive a number of snares and deadfalls to trap or stun small-game animals. However, the success rate of these devices is so low they fall into the last-ditch-tactics category. Perhaps a dozen or more of them have to be tended regularly just to secure a single animal every several days.

A snare is a noose-type gadget that can catch almost anything. Rabbits and squirrels are the primary quarry, but fishers, martens, weasels, woodchucks, and others may show up in it. Even bobcats, coyotes, and wolves can be snared in larger nooses. The latter, if not delectable fare, are neverthelss highly edible and should be looked upon as more-than-welcome survival rations.

The heavy-duty 30-pound test nylon fishing line included in the survival kit is adequate for rabbits, squirrels and similar-size creatures. Anything larger dictates the use of wire, for which the wire fishing leader may play an improvisational role, or you may wish to include a special length of snare wire in your kit just for this purpose.

There are two secrets to using snares successfully. First, they should be positioned where animals are most likely to be encountered. Second, the snare must operate smoothly, unfalteringly; only the animal's head should enter the noose and the slightest resistance should be enough to trip the snare mechanism, causing the noose to tighten instantly and jerk the animal off the ground to prevent its escape.

A resilient sapling bent over provides the spring mechanism and two inverted, notched sticks can be engineered to release the spring at the very slightest disturbance. The noose itself should be suspended somewhat off the ground

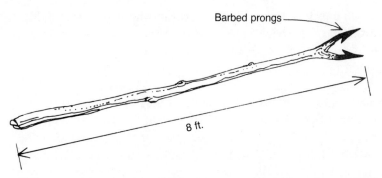

Make your frog gig at least 8 feet long, and hold the prongs briefly over a fire to harden them. The gig can be used to capture fish.

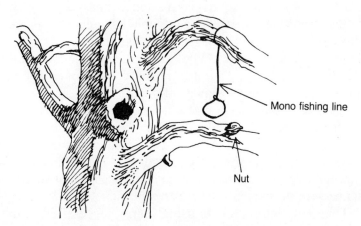

Place squirrel snares on limbs in front of den holes.

at the approximate height of the intended quarry's head by draping it lightly over adjacent bush tips.

By examining the terrain carefully, you can easily find the trails of small game; they generally are trampled paths through tall grass or worn avenues between dense stands of brush or jumbled rock formations. Pick the narrowest place in the trail for your snare, or artificially create a restricted passage that still looks natural, by the strategic placement of brush or branches. Other places to set snare traps are at the entrances to dens, burrows, caves, hollow tree trunks, and similar hideaways frequented by small animals. Snare loops can even be fashioned in front of squirrel den holes in

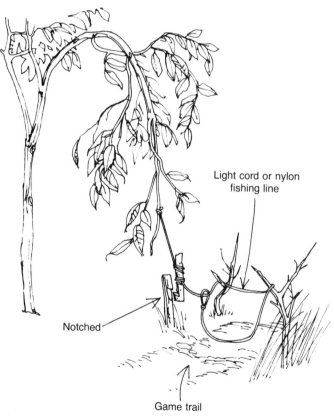

Light cord or nylon fishing line

Notched

Game trail

This effective snare, which will catch almost all species of small animals, is simply a noose suspended over a game trail. Snare is animated by a limber sapling, bent over and anchored with notched sticks which serve as triggering device.

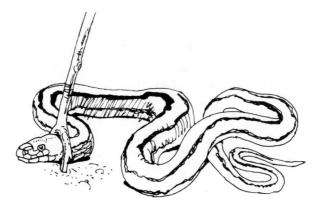

Snakes are easily captured by pinning their necks against the ground with a forked stick.

trees by suspending them from higher limbs and baiting them with nuts.

The deadfall works by enticing a game animal or other creature to a bait station which, when only slightly disturbed, trips a release mechanism that, in turn, causes a heavy log to fall on and kill the animal. The bait itself may consist of almost anything that is highly aromatic, such as carrion, fresh meat, roasted roots or nuts, or whatever else might be available.

Birds. Most survival authorities seem to agree the most consistent way to bag birds is with either a stick-noose or a bola, although many species of ducks and geese can easily be killed with clubs during their flightless molting stage.

The stick-noose gambit capitalizes upon vulnerable blue grouse, spruce grouse, and ptarmigan that in remote areas show little fear of people and remain perched on tree branches even when someone approaches quite closely. Cut a long (10 foot) sapling and make a sliding noose at the tip with a tag end of line extending down the handle. Then, approach quietly and simultaneously slip the noose over the bird's head and quickly jerk it closed. In some cases, these

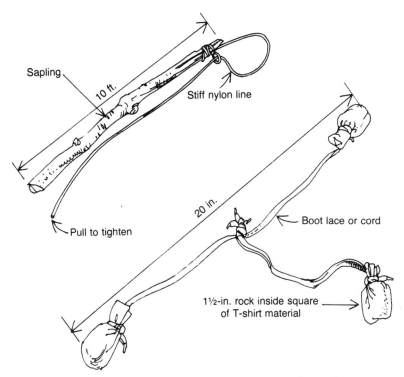

In the wilderness use a long stick with a noose at the end to snare birds sitting on tree branches. If waterfowl are near, fashion a *bola* that can be thrown to entangle their legs and wings.

trusting birds can even be killed with branches or thrown rocks.

A bola is a device consisting of three cords with a rock attached to each. Thrown, it delivers a stunning blow or tangles in the bird's legs and wings to bring it to the ground. You can make a bola by cutting three pieces of material from your T-shirt, each 3 inches square. Lay a rock 1½ inches in diameter in the center of each square. Now take a 20-inch length of cord (a boot lace is ideal) and tie each end to two of the rocks held pouchlike in the T-shirt material; knot the line around the neck of the material. Take a second length of cord and tie one end of it midway along the length of the first, at the opposite end bind the material with rock enclosed in the same manner as before.

A bola is thrown by swinging it around your head as you would a cowboy's lasso, the rocks twirling like a three-bladed propeller at the time of release. For maximum results, use a bola on a tightly grouped flock of ducks or geese while they are resting on the ground or water, or just as they begin lifting off.

COOKING SMALL GAME AND BIRDS

Dressing gamebirds, waterfowl, and small animals is common knowledge so I won't get into it here, but instead will discuss the many ways the resulting pieces of meat can be cooked. A rabbit, for example, can be prepared whole by impaling it lengthwise on a long green stick and roasting it over an open fire. Since a whole rabbit can be rather heavy to hand-hold during the lengthy cooking process, use the reversed forked-stick trick and remember to turn the spit occasionally to expose the entire carcass evenly to the heat of the fire.

Small animals or birds can be quartered and the resulting pieces skewered on pointed sticks and broiled. With any meat, however, be sure to cook it only to the point of being rare because overcooking makes it tough and sacrifices many nutritive values. In fact, many stalwart survival experts denounce open fire cooking, claiming that boiling is far and away preferable for preparing almost any type of food. Not only does this method retain as many vitamins and minerals as possible, they say, but it also wrings every bit of meat and juice out of the carcas. The resulting rich, warm soup also does wonders for your mental outlook in a survival situation.

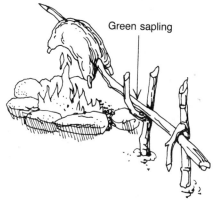

Green sapling

An easy way to roast meat over an open fire without utensils, or even to bake bannock, is by impaling the food on a skewer made from a long green stick. To hold the food in place over the coals, use the reversed-forked-stick trick shown here.

If you are fortunate enough to have an excessive quantity of fish or game one day, and the weather is not cold, you can preserve the additional food by "jerking." This is simply an air-drying process whereby fish carcases are split, or meat sliced into thin strips, and hung over sticks. The meat is ready for storage in your pack after one or two day's exposure to the sun when it has taken on a leathery texture.

Don't discard the hearts, livers, tongues, brains, or kidneys of birds or game animals; all are highly edible. (The exception is the liver of the polar bear, which is so atrociously high in vitamin A it is poisonous to humans.) In the case of fish, retain the livers and any evident roe sacks.

The long leg bones of animals contain marrow unequalled in caloric value by any other natural food. Crack the bones together and roast only briefly over an open fire before removing the marrow with the tip of your knife.

All bird eggs are edible, either raw or boiled in water, so always be on the lookout for nests.

If you catch more fish or game than you can eat at one sitting, dry it for future use. It will be a bit chewy but still very filling and nutritious.

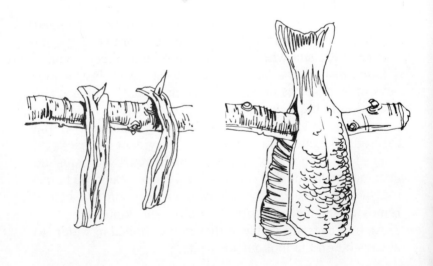

294

Final survival tips to keep in mind:

- Drinking animal blood may seem repulsive, but in critical survival situations keep in mind only four tablespoons of blood provides iron and other important minerals equal to ten chicken eggs.
- Avoid eating toads, salamanders, and gila monsters; they have poisonous glands in their skin.
- Don't eat caterpillars, moths, or butterflies.
- No matter how thirsty you are, drinking saltwater, or your own urine, will only make matters much worse. Better to go entirely without drinking and hope for the best.

▲▲ 17 ▲▲▲▲▲▲▲▲▲▲▲▲▲▲▲▲▲▲▲

Squeaky Clean

Over the years a lot of misconceptions have surrounded the craft of outdoor cooking. One glaring illustration is the tired, overworked tip about rubbing a bar of soap on the bottoms of pots and pans prior to cooking over an open fire. I'll admit the advice has a twinge of merit for those who dislike scrubbing carbon black from the utensils when the cooking is done.

Actually, most experienced trail cooks go ahead and let their pots and frypans blacken. Other than a cursory wipe to remove loose carbon residue, they pay their ebony-stained cookware little mind. The reason is not laziness: the carbon buildup distributes the heat more slowly and evenly, making foods far less likely to burn. Aluminum is too thin and not porous enough to take heat slowly and conduct it uniformly. About the only real saving grace of aluminum is its light weight.

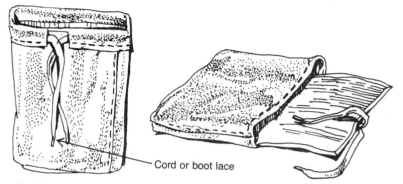

Cord or boot lace

Stuff bags for cook kits, utensils, and other cooking implements can be purchased in camping-supply stores. Or make your own from denim.

So let your pots blacken as they will and in time you'll notice your cookware is doing a far better job than when it was brand new. Just remember to use a factory- or home-made stuff sack with a drawstring to keep your cook kit from dirtying everything it comes in contact with inside your pack.

Another delusion about camp-kitchen clean-up work is that soap makes things clean. This gives soap far more credit than it deserves. Soap is an emulsifier, meaning it has the ability to break down grease molecules and loosen food particles from cookware and eating utensils in order to hasten their removal. But soap is not able to sanitize or kill germs. Consequently, a kettle or dish may look clean, but countless microscopic bacterial organisms may still remain that can easily cause upset stomachs or diarrhea.

Aside from these germs, the soap residue itself can be detrimental to your intestinal constitution, claims my friend Whitey Ellard. Whitey, who not only is a notable trail cook but also a chef in a restaurant in St. Paul, Minnesota, recently explained to me that practically all good restaurants use very little soap in their kitchens.

"Most people falsely equate mounds of suds with spot-lessness," he told me, "but in the restaurant trade we know that the more soap you use, the more difficult it is to remove during clean-up operations, and only a slight hint of soap residue can easily give a customer an acute belly ache. You probably know someone who once ate in a restaurant, or even at home, and later complained of food poisoning, mistakenly thinking the food he ate was spoiled. But in this day and age, with all manner of preservatives and chemical additives in food, spoilage isn't a very common occurrence. What probably happened was the guy or gal ate from a plate or fork that was not entirely rinsed of every speck of soap residue and that's what made him sick.

"Most restaurants generally use just a minimum of soap to cut grease, followed by several thorough rinsings in clear water. Next, and this is the real key to clean cookware and utensils, we slide our trays of pots, pans, dishes, and silver-ware into a steam bath where they are subjected to very hot temperatures. On the trail, you can kill bacteria and germs the same way by dousing your cooking gear in boiling water. If you don't, it's not really clean."

LIGHTWEIGHT CLEAN-UP SUPPLIES

Since profuse amounts of soap aren't necessary or recommended, trail cooks need only bring along some concentrated liquid in a small plastic squeeze tube. Use it sparingly to remove grease and food juices, then rely on other dish-washing measures.

When water is scarce, add just ½ cup to a dirty pot or frypan and then a handful of dirt or sand. Simply use your hands to scrub the pot clean with the abrasive; mix. The gritty nature of common dirt will scour any pot clean of the most caked-on food residues. Of course, you'll not want to

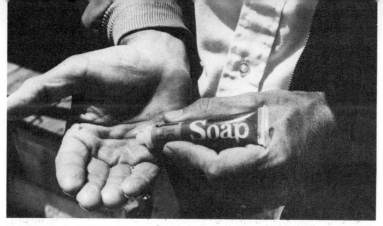

Soap will not kill germs or sanitize cooking utensils. It only serves as an emulsifier to help remove food particles and break down grease molecules. So use it sparingly in concentrated form, then sterilize your cookware and eating gear with boiling water.

use this technique with your Teflon-coated surfaces (they don't need abrasive cleansing, anyway), but for all other cookware and eating utensils, it's nothing short of pure shrewdness. When you've removed the food remnants, throw away the dirt, fill the pot with water, bring it to a boil, and slide in your eating plates, cups, and utensils to sterilize them.

For those who can't bring themselves to wash dishes with dirt, a scouring pad is the next best bet. I find that soap-impregnated steel-wool pads begin to rust after two days or so, and leave you to contend with sudsy bubbles, as well. Instead use a fine-mesh, copper scouring pad which contains no soap, wrings dry after use, and won't rust.

A speedy way of sanitizing plates and eating utensils when there are several members in the party, and a large nested cooking kit is being used, is for each person to have a nylon-mesh "dunking bag." The 1-gallon size that some fruits and vegetables come in is ideal, or you can make bags from nylon-mesh fabric. To use, bring a large kettle of water to a rolling boil while each camper scrubs his own eating gear with sand or a scouring pad. Then put plates and utensils in the nylon bags and slosh them around in the

You can even wash dishes without soap. Simply make a paste of mud and water to scour the utensils free of grease and food, then rinse in boiling water.

For those too squeamish to use mud for cleaning cookwear, use an abrasive pad made of copper mesh. Avoid those of steel wool and impregnated with soap.

To sterilize cookwear, place dishes in a nylon "dunking bag" and submerge in boiling water. Later, hang the bag from a tree limb to drip-dry.

boiling water for a minute or two, holding onto the bags' cotton drawstrings so fingers are not burned. Afterward, the bags can be hung briefly from a convenient tree branch to drip dry, thus eliminating the need for dish-drying towels.

When going it alone and using a small one-man cooking kit, first scrub away grease and leftover food. Then fill the largest vessel you have with water and bring it to a vigorous boil for several minutes. Then to the cauldron add your coffee cup, knife, fork and spoon and let the water come to a boil a second time. Remove the coffee cup and eating utensils with pot tongs and set them aside to drip-dry. Finally, slowly pour the boiling water from the kettle into your concave dinner plate and let it sit for several minutes before discarding.

In disastrous cases in which bean dishes or other foods have become so burned or baked on that they cannot be cleaned by ordinary means, the only solution is to boil the food off. Fill the crusty pot with water, bring it to a boil, and let it perk away for ten minutes. The food will slowly begin to disintegrate. You can add a handful of fine gray ashes from your fire; the mineral salts they contain will help dissolve food and grease in the same way soap does. One thing to remember, however, is never boil water for prolonged periods in a cast-iron utensil, and never use a scouring pad; both will ruin the seasoned finish. The only remedy here is carefully chipping away at the baked-on food with the tip of your pocketknife blade, then a quick dousing with boiling hot water to sterilize the eating gear.

DISPOSING OF CAMP REFUSE

The late, great John Jobson, famous for his camping and hunting articles in national sportsmen's magazines for more than thirty years, once penned a column titled "A Lot of Garbage Has Been Written about Trash." It satirized some of the extremes many self-styled environmentalists have been going to in recent years regarding their strict adherence to packing out *all* refuse.

"Such attitudes may be noble and well intentioned," Jobson said, "but they are so far from realistic practicality they fall into the category of mindless mish-mush."

Jobson's point, of course, is that it's not necessary to carry out absolutely everything that is carried into the wilds. What *is* crucial is learning to dispose properly of refuse in camp or along the trail. Many sportsmen, I'm sorry to say, have not learned these fundamentals, with two unfortunate results: many trails and popular hunting-fishing-camping areas look like city dumps; and wildlife, attracted to the pungent aromas of haphazardly buried garbage, dig it up, adding to the eyesore and often to their own ill health.

Dispose of dishwater in a hole dug in the earth. Do the same with food remnants after they have been charred thoroughly in the fire.

The proper way to dispose of dishwater is not by giving it the old heave-ho, as I have seen some people do. Instead, dig a hole at least 12 inches deep, pour the stuff in, wait a few minutes for the soil to absorb it, then fill the hole back.

in with the sod. Be sure to do this at least 50 yards away from any drinking water source, lake, or stream.

There is no need to pack out burnable materials, such as paper, cardboard, waxed paper, cellophane, plastic food bags, or candy wrappers. Thoroughly burn every scrap in your fire pit, and when you break camp restore the fire site to its original appearance, as described in Chapter 8.

Leftover food or scrapings from plates or frypans should not be thrown somewhere in the woods, but you don't have to pack out these garbage items, either. Thoroughly burn them in a hot fire so nothing remains but soot (again, restore the site before you leave). If there is some food that won't burn entirely, char it the best you can and then bury the remains in a deep hole and cover with soil.

Using the fire pit as a makeshift incinerator is beneficial in several ways: The refuse does not become an unpleasant sight for the next party to pass that way; the burned, now odorless garbage will not attract wildlife as will unburned garbage that is buried; and you aren't burdened by having to tote the stuff back to the trailhead.

When burning is impossible — when you're far above timberline, or exclusively making use of a backpack stove and forsaking all fire building, for instance — burying is acceptable if all biodegradable foods and trash are placed at least 2 feet deep in the earth. If such digging is impossible, there is no other choice but to carry out everything that was taken in.

PACKING OUT NONBURNABLES

Trail cooks frequently have in their possession sundry nonburnables. A few items that readily come to mind include sheet-type aluminum foil brought along for making a reflector oven or rolling out biscuit dough, foil wrappers

Nonburnables such as food tins and aluminum foil should be packed out. First scorch them in your fire, then smash them flat and stow them in your empty cracker box or egg carton.

of many freeze-dried trail foods, occasional canned goods, and foods preserved in small tins, and so on.

In all but survival or emergency situations these items should not be disposed of in outdoor recreation areas because they are not biodegradable and will therefore remain in their original states almost indefinitely.

In dealing with nonburnables, I first rinse them with water to remove food residues, then throw them into the fire. They won't burn but will scorch completely free of labels and any remaining food smells. Then I mash them flat with a rock or the heel of my boot and stow them in a plastic bag or the now-empty plastic cracker box or egg carrier in my pack. The scorching process eliminates lingering odors that otherwise may become unbearably "ripe" in a few days—annoying for you and tempting to wildlife. Mashing, of course, compacts the items for easy storage.

Keep in mind that some nonburnables such as sheet foil can possibly be re-used if they are still in good condition. Wash the foil clean, fold it neatly, and tuck it away for later.

In all other matters related to garbage disposal, common sense and self-imposed responsibility are the earmarks of veteran trail cooks.

There is no need to pack out everything that was packed in, but you should know how to dispose of what you leave behind so the campsite looks as natural as you found it.

Appendix 1

Manufacturers and Suppliers of Trail-Cooking Equipment

Sometimes specific equipment items may be difficult to locate because a good deal of trail-cooking gear is manufactured in Great Britain, France, Sweden, Norway, Finland, and West Germany, then imported into this country by wholesalers. They distribute the merchandise through a complicated network of retail backpacking- and camping-supply stores and dealer representatives that often sell lot quantities to specific chain outlets. Consequently, one retail store may have an entirely different selection of gear from another, and depending upon supply, tariff restrictions, and other factors that supply may differ from year to year. However, most outlets should be able to check their buyer's catalogs and order certain items that are not in stock.

Also, check domestic department stores (and their catalogs) — Sears Roebuck, Montgomery Ward, J.C. Penney — for a wide selection of outdoor cooking equipment. Pay a visit, as well, to sporting-goods shops and retail outlets that carry Boy Scout and Girl Scout equipment.

Following is a list of select manufacturers and suppliers of trail-cooking equipment that will send catalogs upon request, along with some common items they offer:

American Water Purification
115 Mason Circle
Concord, Calif. 94520

Portable water purification
equipment

Backcountry Products
P.O. Box 2565
Tuscaloosa, Ala. 35403

Reflector ovens

Beckel Products
P.O. Box 20491
Portland, Ore. 97220

Reflector ovens

Cabela's, Inc.
812 – 13th Ave.
Sidney, Nebr. 69162

Trail stoves, dutch ovens,
knives, canteens, grills,
botas, utensils

Campways, Inc.
12915 S. Spring St.
Los Angeles, Calif. 90061

Cook kits, trail stoves, botas,
utensils, canteens, plastic
bottles, plastic squeeze tubes,
fuel bottles

Chuck Wagon Foods ((09)
780 N. Clinton Ave.
Trenton, N.J. 08638

Freeze-dried backpack foods,
complete meals, snacks, drinks

The Coleman Company
250 N. St. Francis St.
Wichita, Kans. 67201

Trail stoves

Eastern Mountain Sports
Vose Farm Road
Peterborough, N.H. 03458

All manner of trail-cooking
gear, including Swiss Army
Knives, trail stoves, fuel
bottles, Mautz Fire Ribbon,
Metal Match, botas, cook kits,
plastic storage bottles,
utensils, and freeze-dried
trail foods (Mountain
House brand)

Gander Mountain Supply P.O. Box 248 Wilmot, Wis. 53192	Knives, saws
General Housewares Corp. P.O. Box 4066 Terre Haute, Ind. 47804	Cast-iron dutch ovens
Herter's, Inc. Mitchell, S. Dak. 57301	Cook kits, utensils, knives, trail stoves, canteens, saws, axes, plastic bottles, modest number of camp foods
Laacke & Joys, Inc. 1432 N. Water St. Milwaukee, Wis. 53202	Grills, utensils, Mautz Fire Ribbon, Metal Match, tripod grills, cook kits, stuff bags, dutch ovens, plastic squeeze tubes and bottles, trail stoves, Sterno Piggyback Stove, fuel bottles, knives, saws, axes, backpack shovels, canteens, water-purification equipment, home food dehydrators, freeze- dried trail foods (Mountain House and Rich-Moor brands)
L. L. Bean, Inc. Freeport, Maine 04033	Cook kits, utensils, botas, trail stoves, fuel bottles, canteens, plastic squeeze tubes and bottles
Lodge Manufacturing Company South Pittsburg, Tenn. 37380	Cast-iron dutch ovens
Mirro Corporation Outdoor Recreation Division P.O. Box 409 Manitowoc, Wis. 54220	Cook kits, canteens, plastic bottles, wire grills, tripod grills, utensils

Optimus-Princess, Inc.
P.O. Box 3448
Sante Fe Springs, Calif. 90670

Trail stoves, backpacker's
dutch oven, stove priming
paste, fuel bottles

Oregon Freeze Dry Foods
P.O. Box 1048
Albany, Ore. 97321
(5ᵒ³) 926-6601

Freeze-dried backpack foods
and entire meals, trail snacks,
drinks, compressed Space Savor
foods

Palco Products
3017 San Fernando Road
Los Angeles, Calif. 90065

Canteens, cook kits, grills,
water-purification equipment,
utensils, Metal Match, saws,
axes

Recreational Equipment, Inc.
P.O. Box C-88125
Seattle, Wash. 98188

All manner of trail-cooking
gear, including trail stoves,
fuel bottles, Swiss Army
Knives, cook kits, utensils,
grills, canteens, plastic
storage bottles and tubes,
backpacker's shovels, saws,
axes, electrolyte drinks,
freeze-dried backpack foods
and entire meals (Mountain
House, Rich-Moor, Dri-Lite,
Co-Op, Tea Kettle brands)

Rich-Moor Corporation
P.O. Box 2728   (818)
Van Nuys, Calif. 91404 787-2510

Freeze-dried backpack foods
and entire meals, trail snacks,
drinks, Vegelene cooking oil

Wonder Corp. of America
24 Harborview Ave.
Stamford, Conn. 06902

Trail stoves, plastic
bottles and flasks

Appendix 2

High-Altitude Cooking and Adjusting

Menus should be adjusted as the altitude increases because the higher the elevation the less oxygen is available to metabolize food. Consequently, a greater emphasis should be placed upon carbohydrates (sugars and starches) that have simple molecular structures and therefore are much easier to digest than proteins and fats with their more complex molecular structures.

Keep the actual meal items simple, too, because at higher elevations there is a much lower atmospheric pressure, which causes water to boil at a much lower temperature. For example, at sea level water boils at 212°F, but at 10,000 feet above sea level it boils at only 194°F, and at 15,000 feet at only 184° F. What all of this means is that menu items that require boiling water either for cooking or reconstitution will take much longer to prepare at higher elevations.

Generally, cooking times given on most packaged foods and in recipes are geared toward zero-feet elevation (sea level). Trail cooks should therefore lengthen the specified cooking time by 10 percent for each 1,000-foot rise in elevation.

The following chart shows what the increased cooking time would be for food — spaghetti and meat sauce, say — requiring ten minutes of cooking time at sea level.

Elevation	Required cooking time
Sea level	10 minutes
1,000 feet	11 minutes
2,000 feet	12 minutes
3,000 feet	13 minutes
4,000 feet	14 minutes
5,000 feet	15 minutes
6,000 feet	16 minutes
7,000 feet	17 minutes
8,000 feet	18 minutes
9,000 feet	19 minutes
10,000 feet	20 minutes
11,000 feet	21 minutes
12,000 feet	22 minutes
13,000 feet	23 minutes
14,000 feet	24 minutes
15,000 feet	25 minutes

With this, you can readily see that a common spaghetti recipe requiring only ten minutes' cooking time, as stated on the package, actually requires more than twice that long at an elevation of 15,000 feet. A meal requiring only five minutes' preparation time at sea level would see an increase of only thirty seconds for each 1,000-foot rise in elevation. Each trail cook has to calculate all of his cooking times based upon how far he has ventured into the high country.

How does a trail tramper determine the altitude in order to adjust the required cooking times of the foods? Simply by finding his location on his topographical map. All such maps have various numbers inserted within their contour lines that indicate the number of feet each contour level is above sea level. For example, a contour line with the number 8950 means that specific location is 8,950 feet above sea level. For simplicity, round off the numbers when making your calculations. (In this case, we'd use 9,000 feet, which, for a meal ordinarily requiring ten minutes' cooking time at sea level, would require nineteen minutes.)

One exception to all of this pertains to meats. While those cooked in soups, stews, sauces, casseroles, and other hot liquids take appropriately increased cooking times, *meats cooked in ovens (such as dutch ovens, backpack ovens, or sealed foil containers in reflector ovens or buried in coals) are not affected in their required cooking times by high altitudes.*

Also keep in mind when increasing cooking times that many individuals vary as to their tastes and preferences regarding many foods. In the case of many soups and stews containing vegetables, for example, I like to decrease the cooking time slightly because I prefer vegetables a tad on the crunchy side.

So experiment a little. If a particular recipe requires ten minutes' cooking time, and you're at 9,000 feet, you know you'll have to increase the cooking time by perhaps as much as nine minutes. But once you have passed the ten-minute mark, begin making taste tests every two minutes to make sure you don't overcook the meal. You can always put the stuff back on the burner for a few minutes if it's not quite done, but if it's overly done, there's no going back in the opposite direction.

Lower atmospheric pressure at higher elevations also affects the use of baking powder and baking soda and the rising characteristics of breads and other baked products. Naturally, if there is less atmospheric pressure to push down on the food, it will rise more easily and require less soda or baking powder than at lower elevations where the atmospheric pressure is greater. A biscuit recipe that calls for 1 teaspoon of baking powder at sea level will cause the same biscuits to blow up like basketballs (well, not quite) at 10,000 feet.

Unfortunately, there are no specific guidelines regarding the use of baking powder or baking soda because individual baked-goods recipes vary so much. (Whether you use white flour, whole-wheat flour, pastry flour, Bisquick, or mixtures and whether they are high-gluten or low-gluten make a difference, too.) Follow any given recipe as stated when baking at sea level to about 5,000 feet of elevation. Beyond 5,000 feet, *decrease* the specified amount by about twenty-five percent; beyond about 9,000 feet decrease the specified amount by about half. There are some packers who claim that beyond 12,000 feet they use just a tiny pinch of baking powder or soda, but from my experience this approach works only when using extremely fresh, full-strength, double-acting agents. Otherwise, when you reduce the ingredients so drastically you eventually reach a point where such a small quantity has no noticeable effect.

Furthermore, as elevation increases, the amount of rising time decreases, so following the rising-time allowances in some recipes can be confusing. The best bet, no matter what the elevation, is to keep in mind that the bread or biscuits are ready to be baked when the dough has doubled in volume.

Altitude sickness. Outdoor ramblings in the high elevations sometime result in painful headaches or forms of altitude sickness such as nausea, cramps, or acute fatigue.

The key to preventing this is twofold: First, do not overexert yourself at the outset or allow yourself to become overheated to the extent that you begin to perspire profusely. Give your respiratory and circulatory systems several days, when possible, to adjust to the thin air, and during that time take frequent rest breaks and drink plenty of fluids throughout the day even if you aren't thirsty. Secondly, increase your normal intake of salt in order to keep your body fluid/electrolyte balance on an even keel. I use buffered tablets called Thermotabs, described in Chapter 3, which contain sodium, potassium, calcium, and dextrose. I also frequently take a healthy slug of Gatorade or Gookin-aid ERG (electrolyte replacement with glucose). Others recommend common rock salt, available through any super-market; those who perspire little should swallow, with water, three to five crystals daily, while others who perspire heavily may wish to consume as many as twelve to fifteen crystals daily.

Appendix 3

Common Measures and Weights Useful to Trail Cooks

Measure	Equivalent
60 drops	1 teaspoon
1 teaspoon	$1/3$ tablespoon
3 teaspoons	1 tablespoon
4 tablespoons	$1/4$ cup, or 2 ounces
$5 1/3$ tablespoons	$1/3$ cup
8 tablespoons	$1/2$ cup
$10 2/3$ tablespoons	$2/3$ cup
12 tablespoons	$3/4$ cup
16 tablespoons	1 cup
1 fluid ounce	2 tablespoons
8 fluid ounces	1 cup
1 pint	2 cups
2 pints	1 quart
1 quart	4 cups
1 pound	16 ounces
1 cup	$1/2$ pint
4 quarts	1 gallon

Appendix 4

Selected Additional Reading

Angier, Bradford. *Field Guide to Common Wild Edibles,* 1976, Stackpole Books, Box 1831, Harrisburg, Pa. 17105.

Barker, Harriet. *The One-Burner Gourmet,* 1975, Great Lakes Living Press, 435 N. Michigan Ave., Chicago, Ill. 60611.

Bates, Joseph. *The Outdoor Cook's Bible,* 1963, Doubleday & Co., Garden City, N.Y. 10014.

Bigelow, Howard. *Mushroom Pocket Field Guide,* 1974, Macmillan Publishing Co., 866 Third Ave., New York, N.Y. 10022.

Cardwell, Paul. *America's Camping Book,* 1969, Scribner's, 597 Fifth Ave., New York, N.Y. 10017.

Dalrymple, Byron. *Survival in the Outdoors,* 1978, Outdoor Life Book Club, Box 2016, Latham, N.Y. 12111.

Farmer, Charles and Kathy. *Campground Cooking,* 1979, Digest Books, Inc., 540 Frontage Road, Northfield, Ill. 60093.

Fears, Wayne. *Backcountry Cooking,* 1980, East Woods Press, 820 East Blvd., Charlotte, N.C. 28203.

Fletcher, Colin. *The New Complete Walker,* 1974, Alfred A. Knopf, 201 E. 52nd St., New York, N.Y. 10017.

Herz, Jerry. *The Complete Backpacker,* 1973, The Popular Library, New York, N.Y. 10017.

Knap, Jerome. *The Complete Outdoorsman's Handbook,* 1976, published in Canada, distributed in U.S. by Publisher's Marketing Group, 1515 Broadway, New York, N.Y. 10036.

Marshall, Mel. *Cooking Over Coals,* 1971, Stoeger Publishing Co., 55 Ruta Ct., So. Hackensack, N.J. 07606.

United States Department of Agriculture. *Agricultural Handbook No. 8: Composition of Foods and Nutritional Requirements,* 1978, Superintendent of Documents, U.S. Government Printing Office, Washington, D.C. 20402.

United States Department of the Air Force. *Search and Rescue Survival Manual,* 1970, U.S. Air Force Headquarters, Washington, D.C. 20330.

Index